SCOTT CHROSTEK

ADVENT

A SEASON OF SURPRISES

Market
Square
BOOKS

ADVENT
A Season of Surprises

©2023 Scott Chrostek

books@marketsquarebooks.com
141 N. Martinwood Rd Knoxville, Tennessee 37933
ISBN: 978-1-950899-74-6

Printed and Bound in the United States of America
Cover Illustration & Book Design ©2023 Market Square Publishing, LLC

Cover: Kevin Slimp
Editor: Sheri Carder Hood
Post-Process Editor: Ken Rochelle
Page Layout: Carrie Rood

Scripture quotations taken from the
New Revised Standard Version of the Bible
unless noted otherwise:

NRSV

NIV

MSG

Contents

Introduction

The season of Advent marks the beginning of a new year according to the Christian calendar. For many, the shift from December to January provokes anticipation of new life rhythms created by our New Year's resolutions. Advent is filled with great expectation, too—only the new life it offers us isn't found in trivial resolutions. It's found in new and surprising realities. The season of Advent brings anticipation of what's coming next and points the way to new, authentic life—a life that we could never think to ask for or even imagine. Nobody in the gospel stories leading toward Christmas actually knew what was coming next or to whom it would come. Advent was a beautiful season of surprises.

Do you know what's coming next in your life? In your church? In the world?

I wonder what's coming next for you—beyond the presents, family gatherings, and Christmas traditions? What are you anticipating in your life? What are you dreading?

These are the questions that should fill our hearts and minds during a season like this one, and these are the questions we will wrestle with throughout the pages of this five-week devotional study.

The term "Advent" is derived from the Latin word *adventus*, a translation of the Greek word *parousia,* and it points to something that's on the way. Translated, "Advent" literally means "coming." It's the season of what is to come. We anticipate the coming Christ child, Jesus, or as the prophet Isaiah proclaims, *Emmanuel,* which means "God with us." During Advent, we expectantly await the God of the Universe who is coming to be with us in the flesh.

Have you ever paused to wonder what that means for you personally?

How does God coming to be with us in the flesh change things in our life?

What does it look like to have God with us, and how does that change anything we're facing?

These are just some of the questions the season of Advent evokes, and our answers to these questions will often surprise us! How does the story of Christmas change you? How does a baby born in Bethlehem more than two thousand years ago impact your reality today?

The primary source text for most candlelight Christmas Eve celebrations across the globe comes from the Gospel of Luke in the second chapter. We see Luke's account of what's coming next almost every place you look during the season of Advent. Every nativity scene, most Advent calendars, and almost every children's Christmas pageant tells the Lukan story.

Even if you've never read the second chapter of Luke, you've surely heard it recited word for word while watching *A Charlie Brown Christmas*.[1] Toward the conclusion of that thirty-minute special, Linus (Charlie Brown's thumb-sucking friend) has the Lukan Christmas story memorized as he delivers the closing monologue. The good news of great joy Linus shares comes straight out of Luke. This is the gospel story we long to hear as we await candlelight Christmas Eve services.

However, the season of Advent moves beyond Luke's narrative account of the birth of Jesus Christ and spreads throughout the other gospels as well. The season of Advent includes stories and scripture that allude to realities beyond the birth narrative. Advent is a time to anticipate the Second Coming as well. It's a season that points us toward the cosmic reality of the in-breaking Kingdom of Heaven that is both already (the babe born in Bethlehem) and not yet (Christ's second coming).

---

[1] Bill Melendez, dir., and Charles M. Shultz, *A Charlie Brown Christmas*, CBS, December 9, 1965.

I love how the birth of Christ begins with a closed door in Bethlehem under the cover of night, and the story concludes in Revelation with Jesus standing at the door and knocking. There's something about Advent and the beginning that points us toward the end, which means we reside somewhere in between, in the "already reality" of Jesus but the "not yet reality" of the fullness of his kingdom. Ron Heifitz, in his book *Leadership Without Easy Answers,* would describe that as the difference between the world as it is and the world as it should be.[2] Advent pushes us to anticipate a future filled with hope while, at the same time, forcing us to recognize that we have a lot of work to do to close the gap between here and there; between the world as it is and the world as it should be.

The season of Advent invites us to look for and ponder those chasms or gaps that exist in our present reality; and in the light of Christ, we should strive to close them by living our lives the same way God lives toward us and loves us: with unflinching fidelity and sacrificial love. Advent should provoke us to evaluate the areas of greatest need in our communities and our own lives and inspire us to make changes.

Where are the widest gaps in your city, neighborhood, or family? Where are the widest gaps in your life? Advent charges us to find ways to live, love, and serve

---

[2]   Ron Heifetz, *Leadership without Easy Answers* (Harvard University Press, July 22, 1998).

like Jesus in those places and often in surprising ways.

The God of the Universe is preparing to change the world during Advent, and how God goes about it is truly surprising. God enters our reality in the form of a helpless infant (not a king or ruler). God calls and equips an unlikely couple—whose family wouldn't make room for them—to carry and ultimately deliver the child not in a place of honor but under the cover of night in a common stable, of all places.

As if any of that wasn't surprising enough, upon arrival, God's messengers first reveal this good news of great joy to nightshift shepherds, the lowest of the low (when it comes to shepherds). After that, God leads Zoroastrian priests, people of another faith, to be among the first to visit this helpless child, not kings or rulers. Finally, Anna (a grieving widow) and Simeon (an elderly man searching for meaning) are among the first to recognize Jesus for who he is—perhaps the least likely in the bunch to do so. Nothing happens as it should. The story of Christmas is full of plot twists and holy surprises, but it is precisely through this story and this season full of surprises that we discover hope and new life.

I hope you'll spend time reading through these weekly reflections on your Advent journey, wherever you might find yourself spiritually, emotionally, mentally, or physically, and I pray that you will use this Advent as an occasion for deep personal reflection. I pray that you will reflect over your life and who you are now, and at the same time, pray and dream about who you're becoming, namely the person God sees whenever God looks at you. Perhaps one of the greatest surprises of this season is that God sees us just as we are and invites us, no matter what we have done or left undone, to be a part of his season of life-changing surprises.

The surprising story of Christmas invites us to open our hearts and minds to new realities, and it forces us to make room for God's in-breaking power and presence. My prayer is that this might be your experience of God this Christmas season!

Surprise!

The Good and Bad News of Christmas

Now the birth of Jesus the Messiah took place in this way. When his mother Mary had been engaged to Joseph, but before they lived together, she was found to be with child from the Holy Spirit. Her husband Joseph, being a righteous man and unwilling to expose her to public disgrace, planned to dismiss her quietly.

Matthew 1:18-19 (NRSV)

Christmas is one of my favorite times of the year, largely because of the music. I love Christmas music! I know this is a book about Advent and God's season of surprises, but before we get too far into that, I want to take you back a few months and share my surprising love of another holiday: Halloween. I love Halloween!

You might be wondering, "Why?"

I love Halloween because, for me, it is Advent-Eve. I know this is not liturgically accurate, but starting November 1, every year, by the grace of God, I am able to change my radio stations and playlists to "All Christmas - All the Time." From November to

7

January, I listen to the songs of the season, no matter how inappropriate it may seem to the world around me. It doesn't matter that baseball is still playing or that we haven't yet celebrated the saints fully (though I contend they are probably enjoying Christmas music, too); I am all Christmas in terms of music starting November 1.

I want to listen to Christmas music for as long as I can. Christmas songs bring the season and the story to a fuller, richer place for me. Some of the best Christmas songs come straight out of scripture. To illustrate the point, a crisis unfolded in the midst of Advent a few years back. A mass shooting occurred in a school, and just days before Christmas, our screens were flooded with images of children suffering and crying. Parents were terrified and grieving, and most of the nation was reduced to weeping rubble. In the depth of our pain, Zechariah, the father of John the Baptist, shares one of the best and most surprising songs of the season. He sings:

> *By the tender mercy of our God, the dawn from on high*
> *will break upon us, to give light to those who sit in*
> *darkness and in the shadow of death, to guide our feet*
> *into the way of peace.*
> **Luke 1:78-79 (NRSV)**

Zechariah's song speaks of God's ability to roll back the clouds of darkness and illumine our path so that we might walk in the ways of peace even when that seems impossible. This was a song that we all needed to hear in

8

that particular moment, but it is also a song we should listen to as often as we can. This is why I love the songs of the season. The surprising promise of a holy infant so tender and mild can be felt so purely through the lyrics of a song.

Mary's Magnificat works this way. Mary's song reminds us that in unexpected places and circumstances, God chooses us. God consistently meets us with a strong and mighty arm, and lifts the lowly, selects the insignificant, and redeems the lost with the promise of a future filled with hope. We should sing this song always. It's not just Zechariah and Mary who sing during the season of Advent; it seems that everybody sings all throughout the Christmas story.

The in-breaking power and presence of God at Christmas are so powerful that it often leaves us singing in response. And there is power in the songs of the season. We can find comfort and joy through music.

How does music impact you?

Music has always touched my soul in ways that words or sights never could. I love the melodies, the harmony, the chords—all of it. (Secretly, I've always wanted to play bass!) But what I like most about music is its rhythms and patterns. I love the movement in a song, from its beginning to its end. I love how each chord builds upon the next and how each movement resolves the one before it. Music, like Christ, ushers in a certain type of resolution for my life.

Kurt Vonnegut once wrote:

No matter how corrupt, greedy, and heartless (this world) may become, the music will still be wonderful. Let this be my epitaph: The only proof he needed for the existence of God was music.[3]

Do you know what I like about Jesus? Like a good song, Jesus never seems to let any of us fall unresolved or incomplete. Jesus rescues, saves, delivers, redeems, and makes us whole. Perhaps, that is why some call God the "song of life." Maybe that is why we sing "Blessed Assurance" so much in worship. "This is my story, this is my song." Maybe that's why we refer to God as the beginning, the ending, and all that's stuffed in between. God works through it all—the confused seasons and stanzas of our lives—and, more importantly, God brings about resolution. "We know that all things work together for good for those who love God, who are called according to his purpose" (Romans 8:28 NRSV). God brings forth beauty from ashes. God, just like a good song, never lets us fall incomplete.

In his book, *Resounding Truth: Christian Wisdom in the World of Music*, theologian Jeremy Begbie shares how most songs take us on a journey:

---

[3] Kurt Vonnegut, *A Man without a Country* (Seven Stores Press, September 15, 2005).

They begin in a home key, followed by a move away from that key, and then return to the melody in that home key, but the homecoming is never a simple "back to the beginning." Even if the destination is a note-for-note repetition, it always marks the culmination of a kind of sonic journey, so it will be heard as different—as fuller and richer.[4]

Through music, we can experience the presence of God as God takes us on a journey that starts at home only to return home by the journey's end—only the return home is always better than it was in the beginning. It's fuller and richer than when we started because the road to get there is never easy. It's almost always full of surprising twists and turns, and those surprises work together to build anticipation or a deep longing to return home, so much so that when we eventually get there, it's always better than it was in the beginning.

You see this kind of journey all throughout scripture. If you look at the entire story of scripture (not just Advent), you'll see evidence of this type of journey. In Genesis, we start out in a garden (the garden of creation) only to go on a surprising journey away from the garden on account of our sin and shortcomings. On account of God's grace, the song doesn't end there; the journey continues until we eventually make it back home, to the garden again, only this garden is called paradise, the new heaven and the new earth.

---

[4] James Begbie, *Resounding Truth: Christian Wisdom in the World of Music* (Baker Academic, December 1, 2007).

You see this same journey in miniature throughout the Old Testament. We move with God's chosen, Israel, from the Promised Land into years of wandering in exile, and then from the wilderness, we eventually return home to the Promised Land, the land of milk and honey.

In the New Testament, the Prodigal Son travels away from home, squandering his inheritance in a land of confusion, exile, swine, and prostitutes, only to return home to a heightened sense of what home actually is: a forgiving father, amazing grace, and a giant party.

This same pattern applies to our life of faith as well. Most of us begin our lives with a Sunday school-style understanding about who God is and how God works. Then we venture away from our faith—sometimes in our late teens or twenties—only to come back when we have children of our own. And as children lead us back home, it is fuller and richer seeing God through the eyes of our children. But perhaps it happens more frequently than that. Maybe this kind of journey happens every Advent.

During Advent, we start out with great intentionality only to move away from God by getting caught up in things like excessive shopping, too many obligations, family fighting, clashing politics, and college bowl games. Yet, somehow, by the grace of God, regardless of how far gone we get, God graciously pulls us back in with heavenly peace, candlelight, and the sounds of "Silent Night" on Christmas Eve.

I think this is why we like to sing so much: the movement and rhythm of God's presence in our lives are embedded in the songs we sing. Songs—like God— take us on a journey, and those journeys will always lead us back home, to the beginning, only better. And can I tell you, this is something Joseph (Mary's fiancée) was hoping for.

Not only do we get a sense of unresolved notes and chords in Matthew 1, but we also get the sense that Joseph, a central figure in the nativity, desired more than anything to go back to the beginning to a simpler place and time.

When we encounter Joseph in the Christmas story, we learn that he is about to marry the woman he loves. Like many young men of his day and ours, Joseph was looking forward to a future filled with all those great things like kids, careers, upward mobility, etc. His whole life was ahead of him, and the future looked pretty bright and straightforward.

Then Mary enters the picture, and I'm sure you've heard it a thousand times. Mary was a young, unwed woman engaged to marry this righteous man from the line of David—you know, the one who slayed giants. Mary and Joseph were a perfect couple. He was a carpenter from a strong line. She was a virgin. All systems were a go. And then Mary shared her surprising news.

She was pregnant with someone else's baby. Wait—what?

I imagine it going something like this: Joseph sees Mary walking his way.

Mary says, "Joseph, can we talk? I've got some news to share. Some of it is good news, and some of it is bad."

Joseph responds, "Okay, Mary, let's start with the good news."

To which Mary responds saying, "Joseph, I'm carrying a child."

"Okay. So, what's the bad news?"

Mary replies, "It's not yours."

Come Christmastime, I find myself singing, "Oh, the weather outside is frightful." I believe Joseph would've preferred frightful weather to Mary's news. His was a different kind of fright; his was more personal. Imagine for a moment that the love of your life just shared news of her pregnancy with you, knowing full well that there was no way it could be yours. This would be a game-changer to say the least.

Forget the believability and legitimacy of the story for a moment. Just imagine the experience of learning this kind of news. Can you imagine how you might react?

This was tough on Joseph, for sure—but he wasn't alone. This was tough on Mary as well. Mary was

14

facing a future where she would be known by all her friends and family as the unfaithful woman marrying the faithful man. What if you were known as the impregnated virgin? Who would believe that? Can you imagine the looks you'd receive? Actually, forget the looks; there were actual consequences for actions like these. Joseph, being a righteous man, knew this full well.

Mary and Joseph were engaged, and this was a binding arrangement. They were already legally considered husband and wife. So, this unfaithfulness was actually considered to be adultery. And adultery was resolved one of two ways: death or divorce.

Joseph had a decision to make.

Joseph could either divorce Mary or put her to death. The penalty for infidelity was capital punishment or at least severe and humiliating treatment. Being the righteous man that he was, Joseph knew this. However, Joseph was also a young man in love. He was engaged to be married to Mary. She had his heart, all of it. So, in Matthew's gospel, Christmas begins with Joseph, who is broken-hearted, afraid, and at a complete loss for how to proceed. His future, their future, is hanging in the balance. It was confusing and complicated. I can assure you; he didn't feel much like singing.

I imagine he wondered what would be better for Mary. I imagine he weighed that against what would be better for him, and then perhaps he would have also imagined

what would have been better for them together. He knew
there were two options—divorce or death—but neither
was good. It probably felt like an unresolved chord.

This is what happens next:

> *When (Jesus') mother Mary had been engaged to Joseph,
> but before they lived together, she was found to be with
> child from the Holy Spirit. Her husband Joseph, being
> a righteous man and unwilling to expose her to public
> disgrace, planned to dismiss her quietly.*
>
> **Matthew 1:18-19 (NRSV)**

People talk about dilemmas having two horns; it was
all horns for Joseph. *Either horn he sat on, he was going
to get a sore seat!* He could divorce her publicly, divorce
her quietly, dismiss her publicly, or dismiss her quietly.
Either way, he had to leave her. No way out. No possible
resolution that could lead to a redemptive resolution.
Only pain. So, he planned to dismiss her quietly. He
thought that was his best option.

I don't think he could imagine Mary's story as
believable. I don't think it ever occurred to Joseph that
Mary's pregnancy might be God's truth. I don't think it
ever occurred to him that the only thing lacking might
be his embrace, his acceptance, or his coming around to
a new understanding of who God is and how God works
in the world. He wasn't ready for that yet; he was stuck
in the land of limitations and negative options. He wasn't
open to God's surprising power and presence.

16

After deliberating, discerning, and praying, Joseph went to sleep with his mind made up. He was going to dismiss her quietly, and that is when the story gets really good. Just when he thought he had it all sorted out, God enters in with his surprising resolution.

In his darkest moment, on the darkest night of his life, Joseph goes to bed, prepared to take action in the morning, and God meets him in a dream. Just like the Joseph of old who couldn't help but meet God in his dreams, this Joseph fell asleep and began to hear the angels singing a song of hope.

"Joseph, son of David, do not be afraid to take Mary as your wife, for the child conceived in her is from the Holy Spirit. She will bear a son, and you are to name him Jesus, for he will save his people from their sins." All this took place to fulfill what had been spoken by the Lord through the prophet:

> *"Look, the virgin shall conceive and bear a son, and they shall name him Emmanuel," which means, "God is with us." When Joseph awoke from sleep, he did as the angel of the Lord commanded him; he took her as his wife, but had no marital relations with her until she had borne a son; and he named him Jesus.*
>
> **Matthew 1:20-25 (NRSV)**

God meets Joseph. God speaks to him. Sings to him in his dreams and paints for him a vision of his future that was previously unimaginable. God creates for him

17

a future filled with hope that surpasses Joseph's earlier dreams. *Don't hesitate to show her mercy, Joseph.* In other words, *Give her a second chance! Take Mary as your wife! The child within her is mine. It has been conceived by the Holy Spirit.*

God's words move Joseph from dilemma to decision, and the pathway is abundantly clear. Joseph wakes up and reverses his decision, doing exactly as the angel commanded him to do. He brings Mary into his home, shows her mercy, and offers her a second chance. Joseph chooses to love her. He decides to be faithful unto her, forsaking all others, no matter what the circumstance, and this makes possible a life that he could have never asked for or imagined. He showed Mary mercy.

Have you ever shown someone mercy?

The prophet Jeremiah describes God's promise of mercy this way:

> *"Behold, days are coming," declares the LORD, "when I will make a new covenant with the house of Israel and with the house of Judah...this is the covenant which I will make with the house of Israel after those days," declares the LORD, "I will put My law within them and on their heart I will write it; and I will be their God, and they shall be My people...for they will all know Me, from the least of them to the greatest of them," declares the LORD, "for I will forgive their iniquity, and their sin I will remember no more."*
>
> **Jeremiah 31:31-34 (NIV)**

18

Jeremiah's words point us toward the good news of Jesus Christ. They remind us that the Christ child comes bearing the ultimate gift of mercy. Christ is our merciful Savior who saves us by his grace and unconditional love, a love that was surely learned because this was Joseph's life song. God met Joseph at his darkest hour and urged him to act mercifully, and Joseph's faithfulness, his act of mercy, makes possible the birth of the one who, in turn, saves us by his mercy and grace.

As we anticipate Christmas during this season of Advent, as families gather and people draw nearer to one another this season amidst the good news and the bad, God meets us and urges us to show one another mercy, to extend forgiveness, and to love one another unconditionally. This is what moves us from darkness into light. This is what moves us from our brokenness into something beautiful. God's mercy moves us from the bad news into the good news of Jesus Christ, and the best part is that God uses ordinary people like Joseph as his instruments in making this possible.

In the season of Advent, God meets us where we are and stirs within our hearts a desire to forge ahead through the darkness—through death, divorce, depression, dysfunction, or whatever else we might be facing—by offering us second chances, third chances, tenth chances to love one another the same way that God first loves us: without condition. And this, God promises, will lead us toward authentic new life, the light of Christ.

One of the things I love about Advent is how surprising it is. Before we ever get to Jesus, we get Joseph at his darkest hour, stuck in a no-way-out situation. God meets him and reveals to him a pathway back home, and that pathway is defined by mercy.

Like Joseph, I imagine, we all struggle with tough situations, and mercy is rarely the sought-after pathway forward. However, it's God's mercy that ultimately leads us home; it's God's mercy that makes possible a future filled with hope.

Joseph was at the end of his rope, far away from home, and God pulled him back in with an angel's song of mercy. This song had the power to interrupt the nightmare visions of accusation and estrangement playing in the backdrop of Joseph's dreams and replace them with a manger scene and visions of a baby boy growing and becoming strong because of God's surprising grace and Joseph's corresponding faithfulness, courage, and mercy.

Questions for Reflection

What is your favorite Christmas song? How does it speak to you? Why?

Have you ever received news that seemed overwhelming and unbelievable (like Joseph did)? How do you react when all options seem negative?

Are you open to God's surprising power and presence?

Where and/or to whom might God be calling you to show mercy?

Singing with Surprising Joy

But the angel said to him, "Do not be afraid, Zechariah, for your prayer has been heard. Your wife Elizabeth will bear you a son, and you will name him John. You will have joy and gladness, and many will rejoice at his birth, for he will be great in the sight of the Lord. He must never drink wine or strong drink; even before his birth he will be filled with the Holy Spirit."

Zechariah said to the angel, "How will I know that this is so? For I am an old man, and my wife is getting on in years." The angel replied, "I am Gabriel. I stand in the presence of God, and I have been sent to speak to you and to bring you this good news.

Luke 1:13-15, 18-19 (NRSV)

Can you remember back to the moment that September morning in 2001 when the Twin Towers fell in New York City? The event defined an entire generation and garnered our full attention. It seemed as though time had stopped, and for months on end, we were swirling around in a cocktail of grief, anger, and fear (with maybe a dash of hope).

Everything shut down or changed significantly,

23

especially in New York. Movies stopped filming on the streets in the aftermath of the terrorist attacks, and this was the case for about a year until one of the most popular Christmas movies of all time came around. Will Ferrell's *Elf* was one of the first films to be shot on-site in New York City following the devastation that happened just one year earlier, and this was an intentional decision by the city and the movie's writers and directors. They wanted this beleaguered city to be a part of this movie, hoping that these shell-shocked New Yorkers might experience the real-life joy of Buddy the Elf, played by Will Ferrell, dressed up in an elf costume. They wanted New Yorkers to be surprised by Ferrell trouncing through the streets dressed as an elf in real life. The writers and directors imagined a city consumed by darkness as having an opportunity to experience the light and life of surprising, childlike joy. This is what happens at Christmas. We look forward to the moment when we can encounter pure joy amid the darkness.

Elf tells the story of a child who was abandoned by his parents at an early age. They leave their child on the doorstep of the local orphanage. One Christmas Eve, during Santa's annual visit, Buddy crawls into Santa's sack of gifts. Unknowingly, Santa takes Buddy back to the North Pole, where Papa Elf and several others volunteer to raise him. As he grows up, he does so in the company of elves, not humans. The whole time he's there, Buddy remains unaware of his status as a human until much later when he learns that his biological father is living in New York, which sets the course for the movie.

Buddy sets out for a long trip; Santa advises him that New York isn't as innocent as the North Pole. Buddy journeys only to discover that the world is not all syrupy sweet. There is a lot of darkness out there. He faces all sorts of things and yet can remain buoyant with elf-like or childlike joy.[5] How do you do in the face of darkness? Diagnosis? Disappointment? Despair?

This seems to be not just a good script for a movie, but it's what rests at the heart of our faith as well. The story of Christmas reveals the God of the Universe who chooses to come and be with us by taking the form not of an elf but a holy infant. God comes to us as a baby born in Bethlehem, under the cover of night, surrounded by farm animals in a first-century parking garage. He doesn't come lying in a bed but in a manger, an animal's feeding trough. Talk about surprising!

Nobody was expecting to see this. Nobody was expecting the God of the Universe to be a helpless child, especially not one from misfit parents like Joseph and Mary, in a town called Bethlehem, under the cover of night, lying in a manger. And yet this is how God chose

---

5   Jon Favreau, dir., *Elf*, New Line Cinema, November 7, 2003.

to enter our world. And what's most remarkable to me is that everybody who encounters this surprising child is filled with joy. Much like Ferrell's *Elf,* this child releases all our sins and fears by promoting a heavenly peace as the silent stars go by. Christmas is a time when we experience the power of a child leading the way toward the life we are all looking for. Jesus does this, Buddy the Elf does this, but so do most kids. Advent reminds us—and Christmas confirms for us—that children lead the way.

In the Gospel of Luke, Jesus often shares his love for little children. He reminds us to turn our attention to the little children always. In Luke 18, Jesus calls children over to him and tells his disciples:

> *Let the little children come to me, and do not stop them; for it is to such as these that the kingdom of God belongs. Truly I tell you, whoever does not receive the kingdom of God as a little child will never enter it.*

Luke 18:16-18 (NRSV)

In Matthew's gospel, Jesus exaggerates his preference for children as he shares with his disciples that the Kingdom of Heaven is made up of these little children. This implies, of course, that we can experience the Kingdom of Heaven when we're in the presence of little children, and I would say that is true.

Children carry with them the element of surprise and

26

often lead us toward the joy of the season.

I have a friend in the ministry who lives in the upper peninsula of Michigan. They have a great children's ministry at their church, which includes a couple of students with special needs. As it were, they were putting on a traditional Christmas pageant, and in the process of assigning roles, one of the boys with special needs demanded a speaking role. So, they pondered which role they might give him. Eventually, they landed on the role of the innkeeper.

For weeks, they rehearsed his one line (which he would repeat twice in the pageant): *"No room at the inn." "There's no room at the inn."*

It came time for the performance, and this boy was ready. His time came as Mary and Joseph walked up to the front desk, and just as they'd rehearsed, the innkeeper spoke his line, "There's no room at the inn." The director sighed with relief. And then, as scripted, Mary continued to plead her case. She talked about how she was nine months pregnant and had traveled so far, without food, without shelter, or without a place to deliver her baby, and as we all know, she had a compelling case. But the lines were the lines, and it was time for the innkeeper's second line. He was to say, again, "There's no room at the inn." But nothing came out. Everybody was paralyzed. I imagine the director and the boy's parents repeatedly whispering, *"No room at the inn, no room at the inn,"* but this boy didn't say anything. He stopped, looked around the room for a while, and then he said out loud, *"I think we can make room for her."*

In the middle of what should have been a predictable pageant, this boy delivered a surprising line. Out of the mouths of children, God can speak a divine word of holy surprise that affords us all an experience of the living God. This is what children do all the time. This is also what surprises do. They breathe new life into our stories and give us renewed hope for greater things yet to come. This is the Advent story. It is a season filled with holy surprises.

During Advent, we anticipate the night when the Word became flesh, a night when God meets us where we are by becoming just like us so that we might become just like God.

However, God doesn't come predictably. Instead, God comes in the most surprising of fashions. He comes to us humbly, unexpectedly, almost imperceptibly, in the form of a newborn baby born to an unlikely couple, in an unlikely place, at an unlikely time.

When I think about the birth of Christ, I think about how things must have felt for everyone involved.

For those who were looking for change, they encountered nothing more than a powerless, speechless newcomer. A baby. No matter how great he may have appeared or would become, this baby Savior had no actual skills on the day of his birth. Whatever salvation he might grant or work out during his lifetime was nothing more than a promise, and whatever teaching he might offer would remain hidden for many years.

For those ordinary, everyday people going about their business, this was a non-event. It was life as usual. Herod was still sitting on his throne, and Caesar still governed from afar. The religious aristocracy was still leading as faithfully and hypocritically as ever before. Even as Christ was born on Christmas morning, the world looked as it did before.

So, how does this baby truly change anything? What are we missing? And yet, as we ask those questions, something huge was happening. There was something giant underfoot, and almost everybody missed it. It was almost too surprising.

In the Christmas story, Jesus chooses, invites, and in most cases, surprises the unsuspecting to have their lives transformed. This culminates in the birth of a child, the babe born in Bethlehem. Children lead the way.

Each year, our church hosts a children's event at the beginning of the Advent season. We call it our "Merry Little Christmas" event. Hundreds of children bring their families out to a Christmas carnival with all sorts of activities, including this year's children's Christmas performance. At our most recent performance, I found myself lost in wonder watching about 150 kids dressed up in costume as animals and angels, all of whom were singing joyfully. There were angels, sheep, cows, donkeys, cats, mice, birds, and dogs, and that's just scratching the surface. Regardless of their role, they were all there to sing and remind us about the joy of this season. It didn't matter what you might have been facing. It was impossible not to get lost in their costumed and carefree celebration.

A few years back, I had a chance to go caroling with my downtown church throughout much of the urban core of Kansas City. I was so reluctant, but my pastor's guilt was strong. I felt obliged to go. With a reluctant spirit, I arrived to encounter more than a hundred people, many of whom had brought their kids adorned with flashing lights, full of hot cocoa, as willing instruments of God's joy. By the time they began to sing, I couldn't help but join in, and can I share that I had the biggest smile while doing it? My heart had been filled with childlike joy. I love remembering that night, that group of carolers, singing and smiling brightly in the middle of the darkness, singing songs of surprising joy. We were like Buddy the Elf in the aftermath of 9/11. We were spreading Christmas cheer with childlike joy, regardless of what was going on around us. We were rejoicing. What if we did that all the time?

What if you tried to embody surprising joy everywhere you travel?

What if you tried to smile and sing while making breakfast, riding the elevator, answering the phone, working in your cubicle, even in those moments when you're engaging in an argument? During a season when most of the world seems weary and worn, what would happen if you found a reason for rejoicing?

The Christmas story is one filled with surprises. It's a story of hope, but you'll discover it is also a story of pure joy—and that's often experienced in surprise.

You see this in Zechariah and Elizabeth's story.

In the days of King Herod, there was a priest named Zechariah. Zechariah was a holy man. He was one in a long line of holy men and women. He married Elizabeth, who wasn't just any girl. She was as holy as Zechariah. Elizabeth was one of Aaron's descendants. You remember Aaron, don't you? Moses' mouthpiece? Aaron was the man who stood next to and spoke for the main man of Israel. Zechariah and Elizabeth were a holy couple, a power couple. Each stood blameless and lived blamelessly in the sight of God. But they were struggling. They weren't smiling or rejoicing because scripture tells us that *"Elizabeth was barren."*

This was devastating for them. Two young people in love, both from long lines of prolific holy men and women, wanted to extend their legacy—in fact, they were expected to extend their legacy. So, they prayed for children. Yet, no matter how much they prayed, they never conceived. Elizabeth was barren. Let me tell you, this word is hard. It is painful, and it is real. A friend once told my wife and me, *"The word 'barren' is as hard and as cold as an ice rink in the middle of winter."* Look, he was right, and my wife and I can attest to that. Anyone who shares in this word knows exactly how cold and hard that reality can be.

By the time we meet up with Zechariah and Elizabeth in scripture, they are officially past their childbearing years, and what's amazing is that, despite their pain and struggle, Zechariah and Elizabeth were able to endure it and withstand the pain. They persevered and continued with a resilient faith. They put one foot in front of the next and continued to do so until one day, Zechariah was offering incense to God, and during worship, an angel of the Lord appeared standing at the right side of the altar of incense.

Rather than rejoicing in the presence of one of God's angels, Zechariah is overcome with fear. The angel says to a cowering Zechariah:

> *Don't be afraid, Zechariah! God has heard your prayers. Your wife Elizabeth will have a son, and you must name him John. His birth will make you very happy, and many people will be glad. Your son will be a great servant of*

the Lord...and the power of the Holy Spirit will be with him from the time he is born. John will lead many people in Israel to turn back to the Lord their God. He will go ahead of the Lord with the same power and spirit that Elijah had. And because of John, parents will be more thoughtful of their children. And people who now disobey God will begin to think as they ought to. This is how John will get people ready for the Lord.

Luke 1:13-17 (MSG)

Zechariah's prayers were answered! For unto him a child was to be born. But rather than jumping for joy, singing at the top of his lungs, or even saying thank you, the doubting and depressed Zechariah, thinking about all the pain and despair this would cause his wife should it not come true, says to the angel, *"How will I know that this is so? For I am an old man, and my wife, well, she's as old as me!"*

Zechariah was so focused on the darkness, on their barrenness, that he couldn't trust enough to be set free by the surprising promises of God. More importantly, he wasn't yet able to sing loudly for all the world to hear or even smile. Not yet anyway. He had too much doubt, or perhaps fear.

Zechariah and Elizabeth weren't alone in their doubt and darkness during Advent. Another figure from the Christmas story was there as well. His name was Simeon, and he isn't as well-known.

Simeon

Simeon is a man who received God's promises early on in his life when he was just a young man. God had promised him that he would live until he had a chance to see and hold onto the Lord's Messiah.[6]

You might imagine how receiving a promise like that would make one feel. I suppose Simeon lived with childlike excitement and anticipation while looking forward to Christmas. I imagine him walking through the world with wide-eyed wonder, always looking for that promised moment, but then the first few hours turned into a few days, and then those days turned into weeks, and then months, until all of a sudden, the years were passing him by. By the time we meet Simeon in scripture, so much time has elapsed that a once young and excited Simeon has become old and dejected. He hadn't much hope left, if any at all. He was barren in a different kind of way.

Even though Simeon had been the recipient of God's promise, so much had happened to Simeon that he was stuck in the darkness and shackled by doubt. Can you imagine that feeling?

It's similar, I think, to singing "O Come, O Come Emmanuel" every week in worship and never having the opportunity to sing "Joy to the World." Could you handle

---

6   Luke 2:25-26

singing "Come Thou Long Expected Jesus" every week in worship on repeat? Or would you get tired and weary?

Simeon had gone from being this faithful boisterous pharisee to becoming a quiet, doubting, potentially despairing disciple who barely managed to put one foot in front of the next. Just like Zechariah and Elizabeth, Simeon struggled to be open to God's surprising visions.

The Shepherds

Then there were the shepherds in the field: the lowly, the downtrodden, the perpetually poor. They were the wandering and wondering class of society who faithfully tended to their sheep always and everywhere. Lonely and lost most of the time. These folks were perpetually lost in the darkness, often talking only to their sheep.

Mary

And, of course, how can you forget about Mary, Joseph's future bride? She was confronted by the angel of the Lord with the surprising promise of a child during her engagement. The surprise, I suppose, was that this child would not be Joseph's—which means that God's promise was ultimately sufficient grounds for putting her to death. Needless to say, Mary was not rejoicing— at least not at first. She was scared, alone, and left to struggle with what lies ahead.

All of these characters had their own stories of struggle and perseverance, and none of them were able to rejoice, sing, or celebrate on account of God's surprising visions. Each one was surrounded, if not overwhelmed, by the darkness, even though God had offered them each a surprising vision or promise. They couldn't get past their present predicament, that is, until they encountered a child. Until they saw a holy infant.

Zechariah's story changes when he finally sees that his wife has given birth to their child. Not only does Zechariah learn to speak again after being rendered speechless for months, but with his very first words, he sings! And he sings a powerful song:

> *By the tender mercy of our God, the dawn from on high will break upon us, to give light to those who sit in darkness and in the shadow of death, to guide our feet into the way of peace.*
>
> **Luke 1:78-79 (NRSV)**

Zechariah sings and speaks of God's ability to roll back the clouds of darkness and illumine our path so that we might walk in the ways of peace. This song and that proclamation give us the ability to rise and sing even when we're surrounded by darkness. This is the promise of a holy infant so tender and mild expressed in a song.

Similarly, Mary receives a surprising greeting from her cousin, Elizabeth, and more specifically, from the child in her womb as John leaps. Mary can't help but start singing in response!

36

Simeon sings a song of reconciliation and restoration the second he sees the Christ child in the temple. And the shepherds rejoice, giving glory to God in the highest heaven and peace and goodwill on earth. This is "The First Noel."

James Howell writes:

> *Praise and singing is our best counter to evil in the world. If we are "lost in wonder, love, and praise," there is not much chance we will stumble into tawdry sin, or find ourselves jaded and cynical. Praise is the cure for despair and loneliness. If we "make a joyful noise to the Lord" (cf. Psalm 100:1), we experience a quiet in the soul and a community of love.*[7]

There is power in singing—and I think that's why almost every Christmas movie seems to end with singing because this child stirs within us a desire to be set free. All week long, I've had scenes from *It's a Wonderful Life* going through my mind where people give their gifts to George only to start singing with the angels. I am also remembering the scene from *The Grinch* where the whole town holds hands during their darkest hour, singing songs of praise and worship. I've thought about Charlie Brown and how the whole Peanuts gang tilt their heads back to sing "Hark the Herald Angels Sing."

---

[7] https://www.workingpreacher.org/commentaries/revised-common-lectionary/ordinary-33-3/commentary-on-psalm-98-3.

I don't know what you think about these kinds of things. Elves and Christmas, singing and dancing amid life's darkest moments. I suppose sometimes it's a bit too childish or light-hearted, like maybe it's not for you. Or perhaps you've been there and tried that.

But I keep coming back to the idea that this is the season when children lead the way. In them, we can see a glimpse of the Kingdom of Heaven. In them, we can experience surprising joy that oftentimes leads us to sing with surprising joy.

Let me tell you, wherever you might be, I want to encourage you to become like a child or surround yourself with childlike joy, the presence of children. And then try to mimic their free spirit. One of the ways you can do this is to begin (as Buddy the Elf might suggest) by singing. The best way to spread Christmas cheer is by singing loudly for all to hear. Try singing in your car, in the shower, by yourself, or even in public—because singing is powerful.

Paul writes, "For freedom Christ has set us free" (Galatians 5:1 NRSV). Singing loudly allows us to feel free, to let it all go, familiar songs, even more so. This is also what the Christ child does for us. Singing is one of the primary ways in which we can encounter God. Music can take us, fill us, and lead us into an experience of the living God.

In Psalm 98, we read:

O sing to the Lord a new song, for he has done marvelous things…

Make a joyful noise to the Lord, all the earth; break forth into joyous song and sing praises…

Let the sea roar, and all that fills it; the world and those who live in it. Let the floods clap their hands; let the hills sing together for joy at the presence of the Lord.

Psalm 98:1, 4, 7-8 (NRSV)

Songs fill us up and allow us to experience and share in the promises of God. They bring about Christmas cheer for all the world to hear—not just us but the whole world.

John Wesley, the founder of the Methodist movement, loved to sing as well. Singing was one of the ways that fostered his ongoing connection to God. He felt so strongly about singing that he wrote instructions on how to sing. He encouraged his people called Methodists, saying this:

John Wesley's "Directions for Singing":

I.   **Learn these tunes before you learn any others**; afterwards learn as many as you please.

II. **Sing them exactly as they are printed here**, without altering or mending them at all; and if you have learned to sing them otherwise, unlearn it as soon as you can.

III. **Sing all of them.** See that you join with the congregation as frequently as you can. Let not a slight degree of weakness or weariness hinder you. If it is a cross to you, take it up, and you will find it a blessing.

IV. **Sing lustily and with a good courage.** Beware of singing as if you were half dead, or half asleep; but lift up your voice with strength. Be no more afraid of your voice now, nor more ashamed of its being heard, than when you sung the songs of Satan.

V. **Sing modestly.** Do not bawl, so as to be heard above or distinct from the rest of the congregation, that you may not destroy the harmony; but strive to unite your voices together, so as to make one clear melodious sound.

VI. **Sing in time.** Whatever time is sung be sure to keep with it. Do not run before nor stay behind it; but attend close to the leading voices, and move therewith as exactly as you can; and take care not to sing too slow. This drawling way naturally steals on all who are lazy; and it is high time to drive it out from us, and sing all our tunes just as quick as we did at first.

VII. **Above all sing spiritually.** Have an eye to God in every word you

sing. Aim at pleasing him more than
yourself, or any other creature. In
order to do this attend strictly to
the sense of what you sing, and see
that your heart is not carried away
with the sound, but offered to God
continually; so shall your singing be
such as the Lord will approve here,
and reward you when he cometh in
the clouds of heaven.[8]

Do you sing? Are you singing this way? It's hard to do,
but Advent is a season for singing with surprising joy, for
unto us a child is born and a son is given! The God of the
Universe is becoming like us, becoming a child so that
we might be surprised and set free by this good news of
great and surprising joy. Smiling should be our favorite,
and so should singing, and more specifically, singing
loudly for all the world to hear.

I love this time of year because, just above the cash
registers in every store, I can hear the "heavenly music
float o're all the weary world." I love that this little child
sets free children and adults alike amid whatever we
might face individually or collectively. I hope you, too,
will be set free.

*(And now, with all of that said, if singing still isn't for
you, re-read this whole chapter inserting the words "living
differently," "standing out," or "serving others" every time*

---

[8]   *The United Methodist Hymnal* (The United Methodist Publishing House, 1989).

I talk about singing. Perhaps that will allow you to be set free in a way that surprises you and transforms you into the life you're looking for!)

Questions for Reflection

Where do you see yourself in these stories of surprise?
Zechariah and Elizabeth's, Simeon's, Mary's, or even the
shepherds' stories? Are you able to sing? Are you looking
for joy? Are you reluctant in doubt?

This time of year can be difficult. Can you take time to
think of or find reasons to rejoice and share joy with
others? What are your reasons for rejoicing?

When was the last time you were unfettered and free, so much so that you were willing to sing for all the world to hear?

Have you encountered the Christ child yet? If so, describe your experience.

Christmas and its Cast of Misfits

In the sixth month the angel Gabriel was sent by God to
a town in Galilee called Nazareth, to a virgin engaged
to a man whose name was Joseph, of the house of David.
The virgin's name was Mary. And he came to her and
said, "Greetings, favored one! The Lord is with you."
But she was much perplexed by his words and pondered
what sort of greeting this might be. The angel said to
her, "Do not be afraid, Mary, for you have found favor
with God. And now, you will conceive in your womb and
bear a son, and you will name him Jesus. He will be
great, and will be called the Son of the Most High, and
the Lord God will give to him the throne of his ancestor
David. He will reign over the house of Jacob forever, and
of his kingdom there will be no end." Mary said to the
angel, "How can this be, since I am a virgin?"

Luke 1:26-34 (NRSV)

In our first week of this study, we focused on the
dynamic tension found in music and how the unresolved
notes or chords we often experience in life leave us
longing to return home. During Advent, we long
to experience the fullness of God and God's future
filled with hope. The season of Advent culminates on

Christmas as the God of the Universe enters into our unresolved realities with words that redeem us and make this hope-filled future a reality—and it leaves us all singing in response.

That said, have you ever paused to think about the irony of the night when Christ was born? I mean, we're waiting and waiting for a baby—of all things—to change everything. The life of a newborn infant is the light that will pierce all the darkness of doubt and death forever, and really, the only way anybody would ever know that our reality has changed is upon hearing the sweet sound of a baby crying. And we mark the moment by singing, "Silent Night, Holy Night."

That doesn't make any sense to me. Does it make any sense to you? Also, have you ever heard a baby crying in the middle of the night?

As a father of two, hearing a baby cry hardly seems like good news with great joy, and it certainly doesn't seem like a reason to get all worked up and celebrate. Crying babies bring with them a whole range of emotions. For me, it can be paralyzing, and anyone who has tried to quiet a crying baby on an airplane or in a church knows that this is not something to look forward to with great anticipation, or to meet with singing.

Something doesn't seem to fit here. And then again, sometimes during the holiday season, we feel like *we* don't fit in. Sometimes Advent brings with it mixed emotions or conflicting messages. It comes with crying babies instead of "Silent" or "Holy Nights." We get fifty degrees and rain instead of a "Winter Wonderland." Or perhaps we are consumed with grief or fear instead of hope and joy.

Have you ever felt that way? Like things aren't fitting together, like things don't make sense, or that it just doesn't feel like Christmas the way you were hoping it would? If the answer is yes—even if it's no—then perhaps you should turn not to singing (like the last chapter suggests), but to movies instead.

For some, Advent is a season full of great anticipation, and we look forward to celebrating the night Christ was born. But for just as many, Advent is a season where we enthusiastically await the return of our favorite Christmas movies, new and old.

My guess is that you've watched a Christmas movie or two before. In fact, you have probably argued with your friends or family over which movies are the best—and I know you have been a part of a conversation where someone tried to convince you that *Die Hard* is, in fact, a Christmas movie. (For those of you who are wondering, it isn't.)

Whatever Christmas movies are your favorites, we can't seem to get enough of them this time of year. What is your favorite Christmas movie?

One of my favorite Christmas movies is Rankin and Bass' 1964 stop-motion animation classic *Rudolph the Red-Nosed Reindeer*.

47

I've done some digging into the background of Rudolph, and before I jump into this chapter too far, I want to make something abundantly clear: Dasher and Dancer, Prancer and Vixen, Comet and Cupid, and Donner and Blitzen have been hauling Santa's sleigh forever. As far as I can tell, they are the real-deal reindeer, and they have been since the very beginning. Rudolph, however, is another story. The ninth reindeer, the one with the "nose so bright," he didn't come along until one foggy night in 1939 on the heels of the Great Depression.

Robert L. May was an advertising executive working for Montgomery Ward, a large Chicago-based retailer. In 1939, Montgomery Ward had endured some significant financial difficulty due to the struggling economy, but that year, they were gearing up for what would hopefully be a big holiday shopping season. So, the leadership asked May to create that year's Christmas promotion. What many didn't know was that May was also struggling due to his wife's ailing health. She was dying.

With everything weighing on him, the pressure of home, the pressure of the economy, and this Christmas campaign, May was working on an upper floor in downtown Chicago looking out upon the waters of Lake Michigan. Then one foggy night, as May was working on ideas, he peered out the window, and in the distance, he noticed a great light coming from a lighthouse in the distance cutting through the fog like a spotlight. It was in that moment, sitting there in the middle of the fog both personally and professionally, that May got the idea for a ninth reindeer to pull Santa's sleigh, the youngest reindeer, the smallest reindeer, the reindeer who would be different than the rest in a way that would ultimately make possible a future filled with hope no matter how dark or thick the predicament seemed. This is how Rudolph came to be. May saw a lighthouse shining so bright that it cut through one foggy night.

May viewed himself to be like Rudolph, not because he had a bright shiny nose but because he felt like he didn't fit in. He had always felt like a bit of an outcast, a misfit. At thirty-five, he felt far from reaching his potential, and given his wife's health and his career, the future didn't seem bright. Rudolph was May's story.

Nationally, the U.S. was on the heels of the Great Depression and about to engage in World War II, so everything seemed a bit foggy at the time. And so, Rudolph's story really became everyone's story. It was an underdog story about a misfit who would use everything he had to find a way through the fog to live into a future filled with hope.

May's wife passed away from cancer just eight months into the Rudolph project. He became a widower and single father. He was devastated. So his boss offered to take the reindeer project off his plate, but May refused, saying, "I need Rudolph now more than ever."

Apparently, so did the rest of the world.

After the story was published, it grew in popularity. Montgomery Ward distributed over 2.4 million copies of Rudolph in its first year alone. In 1948, it was transformed into a television cartoon. In 1949, May's brother-in-law put Rudolph's story into song form, and they gave it away to a cowboy named Gene Autry, who released it. Within that first year, more than 2.5 million people purchased it. Now there are well over 150 million people who have picked up some version of this song over the years. My guess is that you're a part of that number. It took twenty-five years after the idea was initially born that the made-for-TV movie special became one of the most popular Christmas traditions to this day.[9] I contend that Rudolph's popularity and success are related to how the story of this "different reindeer" lends itself to our experience of the real Christmas story.

One thing becomes clear from the moment the movie starts: Rudolph is a story about misfits. It's all about people that don't fit in our world, our society, our version of how things should be—and we all have our version. If we're being honest, inside every one of us lies the idea that life would be so much easier if everything just fit

---

[9] https://www.npr.org/2013/12/25/256579598/writing-rudolph-the-original-red-nosed-manu-script; https://time.com/5479322/rudolph-the-red-nosed-reindeer-history-origins/; https://www.theatlantic.com/magazine/archive/2020/12/rankin-bass-rudolph-the-red-nosed-rein-deer/616932/; and https://www.cbc.ca/documentarychannel/features/the-real-story-be-hind-rudolph-the-red-nosed-reindeer#:~:text=Rudolph%20the%20Red%2DNosed%20Rein-deer%20was%2C%20in%20fact%2C%20penned,he%20had%20for%20his%20daughter.

together nicely and neatly the way we had planned.

Think about Thanksgiving and the lengths we go to pull off these large, elaborate dinners with the perfect place settings, conversation, meal courses, and football. If only those plans came to fruition the way we envisioned they would. If only everything happened the way we planned and people acted the way we thought they should, life would be better. If only we didn't have to deal with *those* people. You know who they are: the people who don't fit with our plans. *Why did they say that? Sit there? Forget that?*

To be honest, things rarely happen as we imagine, and thank God for that—right, Joseph? We need variety, diversity of thought, gifts, and passion. We need surprises. In his letter to the Romans, the Apostle Paul describes our diversity of gifts as different parts of the same body. We're bound together by one Spirit, but each has different capabilities or roles to play. If we were all the same, if we were all eyes or ears, then things wouldn't work at all. We need each other. We're better together, as misfit as we may seem. But it's easy to forget this—or we choose to forget this. Instead, we focus on our differences and see them as divisive or misfits.

This is the story of Rudolph and Hermey the Elf. They are both misfits. They are different than the rest, the wrong kinds of characters.

We meet Rudolph moments after he's born, and as

far as anyone can tell, he's perfect. His disposition is so sweet and pure. He is smart and knows his mama's and papa's names, but one thing about him gets in the way. He doesn't look like the other reindeer; he has this shiny red nose—and that just can't be. There's no room in this world for a reindeer with a red nose. At one point, his mom says to her husband, *"Oh, we can look past this (his red nose)."* His dad says, *"No, we can't. We can't look past this."* Later he tells Rudolph, *"We're going to have to cover it up."* And they do. They covered up the very thing that made him different, pretending as though it didn't exist. That's how bad it was—or so they thought.

Rudolph's dad was thinking, *If we don't hide his nose, he won't be able to do anything. He'll never be able to pull Santa's sleigh or play with the other reindeer.* Rudolph's dad couldn't imagine a reality where any of that could be possible. So, he forces Rudolph to fit in. It works for a while, I suppose, but you can't hide forever.

Rudolph's red nose eventually comes out, and that's when things get really bad. Rudolph is ridiculed and judged by everybody. It's horrible really. So, he runs away ashamed, feeling like he doesn't fit in anywhere. He is lost and alone.

Another misfit in the story is Hermey the Elf. Moments after Rudolph is ridiculed, we meet up with Hermey, an elf who, unlike the other elves, doesn't like to make toys. He wants to be a dentist. And the same kind of thing happens to Hermey as it did to Rudolph—because there's no room in this world for an elf who doesn't want to make toys. The very thought of it is so troubling or obtuse that it forces the boss elf to fly off the handle. He screams, "Get back to work, or you're fired!"

After giving the toy-making business one more try, Hermey simply can't do it anymore. He eventually leaves the North Pole after being humiliated, laughed at, and judged for his unwillingness to build toys one last time. Hermey, like Rudolph, finds himself lost and alone. He, too, doesn't fit anywhere.[10]

What is it about humanity that it doesn't react well to things that don't fit into our picture of the world?

One might think that everybody should most easily identify with Rudolph or Hermey when watching the film, but the truth is that we struggle with them, too—but I'm not simply talking about the two characters here. We often think to ourselves concerning others, *What's wrong with them? Why do they do that? Why do they think that way? Vote that way?*

Have you ever said any of those kinds of things before?

We tend to judge and criticize those who don't fit into our world. We struggle to accept differences politically,

---

[10] Romeo Muller and Robert May, *Rudolph the Red-Nosed Reindeer*, Rankin/Bass Productions, Inc., NBC, December 6, 1964.

personally, professionally, and denominationally. We can't help ourselves.

This is part of what Rudolph forces us to wrestle with, and this is also what the Christmas story forces us to wonder about as well. The Christmas story is also a story about "misfits." The story of Christmas is about a God who chooses misfits to change the world.

Nearly everybody in the Christmas story is a misfit, and it begins as God appears to Elizabeth and Zechariah. Now, on the surface, these two seem like the right people to effect some real change in the world. Zechariah is a holy man, one in a long line of holy men and women. And Elizabeth is one of Aaron's descendants—Aaron, as in Moses' brother, Aaron. Zechariah and Elizabeth are a holy couple. Each stood blameless and lived blamelessly in the sight of God. But they weren't without struggle. The Christmas story begins as the angel of the Lord appears before this pained couple, misfits in this world because of their barrenness. Yet as they were in their eighties and nineties, the angel said, *Don't be afraid, I'm giving you a child, and you'll name him John. He will be filled with the Holy Spirit and turn many people to the Lord their God.*

I picture Zechariah saying, *What? Surely you have the wrong couple. We're way too old!* And yet, after we talked about in the last chapter, God's promises were fulfilled: Elizabeth gave birth to John the Baptist, who would go on to prepare the way of the Lord. However, it wasn't easy for them. Can you imagine their reality of being pregnant at such an advanced age? Do you think they blended in as brand-new parents? Do you think they were believable as parents or a welcome family at local daycares or early learning centers as they inquired about the potential availability for their soon-to-be child? If you had pulled out Zechariah and Elizabeth's wedding photos and compared it to the photos of their life now with their newborn, you wouldn't even recognize them. They were so old. They were the age of great-grandparents, and yet here they are, invited by God, carrying a child into this world. They were overjoyed, I'm sure, but look, they didn't fit in. They were shunned because they stood out, misfits for the mission at hand.

In the sixth month of Elizabeth's pregnancy, the same angel of the Lord appeared before Mary, Elizabeth's much younger cousin. This is what we read in Luke:

> In the sixth month the angel Gabriel was sent by God to a town in Galilee called Nazareth, to a virgin engaged to a man whose name was Joseph, of the house of David. The virgin's name was Mary. And he came to her and said, "Greetings, favored one! The Lord is with you." But she was much perplexed by his words and pondered what sort of greeting this might be. The angel said to her, "Do not be afraid, Mary, for you have found favor with God. And now, you will conceive in your womb and bear a son, and you will name him Jesus. He will be great and will be called the Son of the Most High, and

the Lord God will give to him the throne of his ancestor
David. He will reign over the house of Jacob forever, and
of his kingdom there will be no end." Mary said to the
angel, "How can this be, since I am a virgin?"

Luke 1:26-34 (NRSV)

Luke does a great job of revealing Mary's awareness in this text. She recognizes the magnitude of God's call and her lack of qualifications for the task at hand. Mary feels like a misfit too. Unlike Elizabeth, Mary is on the opposite end of the age spectrum. She is thirteen, maybe fourteen, and she isn't married yet. Mary is an unwed virgin who is engaged to be married to Joseph. And let me tell you, Joseph was no Zechariah. Joseph was a rather ordinary carpenter from Nazareth, and yet, he is who God chooses to carry his child, the Son of the Most High, whose reign and kingdom would have no end.

Mary says, *How can this be?* God replies, *Look, nothing is impossible with me.* And I suspect that's when things got worse for her, not better.

How do you think people saw her?

She was carrying a child born out of wedlock. The world didn't have room for a person like Mary. She didn't have a red nose; she had a baby bump. Mary was pregnant, and it wasn't Joseph's. This meant that she didn't fit in. She, too, was all alone, a misfit for the mission.

These two women, Mary and Elizabeth, are the first

two central figures in the Christmas story. They are outcasts, and they don't fit in. They are all alone because of their unique God-given gifts. This is just like the Rudolph story.

As Rudolph continues, with both Hermey and Rudolph running out on their own, these two misfits meet up with each other on the journey. They find each other, see each other, appreciate each other, and decide to be independent together. And if you've seen the film, you'll remember that immediately after agreeing to do life together, they break into one of the most notable songs in the movie: "We're a Couple of Misfits!"[11] Their tone and tenor change altogether. The same thing happens to Mary and Elizabeth. They find each other too.

Mary travels from Nazareth to Ein Karem to find Elizabeth, her cousin, and as Mary arrives at Elizabeth's house, the child in Elizabeth's womb leaps for joy. Immediately upon seeing Mary and the gift she's carrying, Elizabeth refers to Mary (her cousin) as the mother of her Lord. Elizabeth blesses her, encourages her, and together they become one with each other, one in mission and ministry to the whole world.

Like Hermey and Rudolph, Mary and Elizabeth set off on this holy adventure together—but not before singing. Just before they leave to embark upon the rest of their

---

[11] Johnny Marks, "We're a Couple of Misfits," *Rudolph the Red-Nosed Reindeer*, Rankin/Bass Productions, Inc., NBC, December 6, 1964.

adventure, Mary sings the Magnificat, one of the most amazing songs in scripture, a song that reminds us all that in places and circumstances unexpected, God meets us, chooses us, and with a strong and mighty arm, God lifts up the lowly, selects the insignificant, and redeems the lost in a way that blesses them—and us—with the promise of a future filled with hope. God chooses misfits to do the extraordinary!

This is what Mary sings:

> *My soul magnifies the Lord,*
>
> *and my spirit rejoices in God my Savior,*
>
> *for he has looked with favor on the lowliness of his servant....*
>
> *He has shown strength with his arm;*
>
> *he has scattered the proud in the thoughts of their hearts.*
>
> *He has brought down the powerful from their thrones,*
>
> *and lifted up the lowly;*
>
> *he has filled the hungry with good things,*
>
> *and sent the rich away empty.*
>
> *He has helped his servant Israel,*
>
> *in remembrance of his mercy,*
>
> *according to the promise he made to our ancestors,*
>
> *to Abraham and to his descendants forever.*

Luke 1:47-48, 51-55 (NRSV)

The "misfit" Mary's song shines through the thick fog of Advent, reminding us all that, with God, all things are possible. God knows what God is doing when God chooses us, delivers us, and makes it possible for us to shine brightly in the world around us. God sees possibilities in us, even when others cannot. Even when we cannot see it ourselves.

And that's what Elizabeth saw when she met Mary. She didn't see an unwed virgin carrying a child outside marriage (like Joseph initially saw). She saw life-changing power and potential, the mother of her Lord.

This is how God sees us. This is how we ought to see each other, as different or misfit we may feel. Instead of seeing our differences as deficits or deficiencies, we ought to see our differences as gifts with great and unimagined possibilities.

The season of Advent is preparing us for something that far surpasses anything we could ever ask for or imagine—and all along the way, we meet up with a collection of unexpected misfits and holy surprises. It involves people like Mary and Elizabeth, Joseph and Zechariah. It involves treacherous journeys over long distances, a baby born in a manger for a bed, and animals for an audience, where wise men and shepherds are the first to bear witness.

Nothing about it makes any sense, and yet, by the grace of God, under the cover of night, shattering our best attempts to control the narrative, God shines a light that pierces the darkness and breaks us free from the chains of our conventional wisdom and control. We have hope and can rejoice the moment we hear a crying baby—because God chooses to enter into our unresolved reality in surprising ways through the lives of unexpected people willing to travel down unexpected pathways that nobody saw coming! That's the good news—because God sees possibilities where others cannot. And listen, God longs for you to see yourself and others in the same way.

People eventually see God's unlimited possibilities in Rudolph as well, but not until the very end of the movie. Blizzard conditions threaten Christmas, and Santa doesn't know what to do, so he plans to call off Christmas. But then he sees Rudolph. Santa finally sees Rudolph for who he is. He sees Rudolph's power and potential. *That nose? That nose! Rudolph, with that nose so bright, won't you guide my sleigh tonight?*

The very thing that made Rudolph an outcast saved Christmas. His red nose was able to cut through the foggy sky. Similarly, Mary's gift wasn't something hide; it was the very thing that would illuminate the entire world. Mary's child was the light that pierced the darkness.

Throughout the years, I've had the privilege of spending time in Israel, retracing the footsteps of Jesus. On these journeys, one of my favorite places to visit is the Basilica of the Annunciation. It's the church over the place where the angel Gabriel shared the news with

Mary, where she received the good news of great joy! I love this chapel because, when you walk into it, nothing in it seems to fit together. It's a misfit too.

These big, rough concrete beams are stamped with large dimples holding this giant, sacred structure together. Between these concrete beams are beautiful portraits of Mary, amazing works of art, and each portrait is different than the next; no two portraits are alike. Each portrait represents a different nation's perspective of Mary, and everybody had a different take.

The longer you stand there amidst the concrete structure and ornate portraits, you eventually realize there are two levels to this Basilica. The upper level houses a modern sanctuary, which sits on top of the lower level and centers upon a cave or dwelling place that dates to the fifth century (the place where Mary received the word). Looking at the two worship spaces interspersed with these giant concrete beams and amazing pieces of art, none of it really makes any sense, except that there's one thing that connects it all. There's a big, open area running up and down the center of the entire Basilica. It spans from the very bottom, below ground, all the way to the very top of the steeple. However, after looking up and down this channel, one begins to realize that the Basilica of the Annunciation doesn't have a steeple; it has a lighthouse. This is the place where the light entered the world, where Mary became pregnant, and nothing about the story made any sense. It was misfit! And yet God seems to make perfect sense out of what we perceive to be nonsense. This was true for Mary, and it was true for Robert L. May as well.

Charged with leading Montgomery Ward out of the Great Depression at the precipice of World War 2, Robert L. May was carrying the uncertain prognosis of his wife's illness. The weight of the world, or what felt like it, descended upon him. As he struggled to devise a pathway forward, he looked out of his Chicago high-rise and saw a lighthouse shining in the distance. From that light came hope and the promise of new life in the storyline of *Rudolph the Red-Nosed Reindeer*, even amidst the foggiest of nights.

As one travels to Nazareth, one will discover a lighthouse shining above the place where the light of Christ became real for us. As hard as it is to accept, the story of Christmas started with a couple of misfits, who, by the grace of God, would prepare the way and give birth to the hope of the nations, so that we might realize that, by God's grace, we have the power to do the very same thing.

So, go and let your lights shine before others so that through your life, your gifts, and your love, you might lead others to experience the life and love of Christmas.

ลง

Another way of looking at the
story of Mary and Elizabeth

When God met both Mary and Elizabeth and shared
with them the news of his selection for their children
and all they would have to endure, nothing in the world
around them had changed. The outside world didn't
know any different. Everything inside their world had
changed dramatically—and not for the better. Once the
two women met God, their lives were turned upside
down. But to make matters worse, their lives were
turned upside down in an undesirable way. They didn't
immediately realize the "good life of social standing
or wealth," nor were their paths made any easier by
God's authority. Mary's new status as an unwed mother
of somebody else's baby warranted the death penalty
or divorce. And upon conceiving at such an older age,
Elizabeth would have been abandoned by her friends.
And one must not forget that Elizabeth's husband
couldn't speak all throughout her pregnancy. However,
Mary and Elizabeth persevered in faith together.

These women, with their newfound surprises and
adversity, join up with one another. They were drawn
to each other by a common experience, and by coming
together, they revealed a new hope for the nations.

The birth of Jesus is a new story with roots in the
past. Toward the end of Luke 1, what we have ultimately

is a story about two baby boys, both in the womb. One is older (Elizabeth's child, John the Baptist), and he is set to usher in the end to an age (by preparing the way for the Lord). The other boy is younger (Mary's child, Jesus), and he will mark the beginning of a new age. In this story, breaking with Jewish tradition, the younger boy will rise above the older boy and usher in something brand new, the fulfillment of all ages, the new covenant of God. However, as unconventional as this story is in that the younger boy would rise above the older boy (Jewish tradition favored firstborns), there is something strangely familiar about it.

The story of Christmas, the season of Advent, is a story that points to the future, a future whose roots are in the past. You can see that in this encounter between cousins, and more specifically, their two babies, John the Baptist (the older child) and Jesus (the younger child). Seeing these two boys in Advent should remind us of Jacob and Esau, twins who also happened to meet in a womb. Both Jacob and Esau wrestled for God's blessing. In that story, Jacob, Rebekah's younger boy (Jacob), eventually rises above the older boy (Esau). Jacob takes the blessing to carry Israel forward into a future with hope. However, their process of blessing included things like deceit, plotting, and jockeying for position. In fact, Esau is enraged at Jacob's deceit. He wanted to kill him. Thankfully, the Christmas story reveals something both surprisingly and refreshingly different.

The Spirit washes over Elizabeth and her son, the older boy, and upon meeting Jesus, the younger boy (womb to womb or belly to belly) leapt for joy. Unlike Esau, who was teeming with jealousy and anger, John the Baptist was rejoicing in the power of the Holy Spirit, all of which caused Elizabeth to rejoice. Elizabeth referred to Mary not as her cousin but as the mother of her Lord, to which end Mary started singing a song as well.

If you slow down to read this story, in the stillness of the moment, you will find differences in the Christmas story that you might not have otherwise seen. And all over again, we find ourselves surprised by God's power and presence in a familiar way. Here at Christmas, the firstborn (John the Baptist) rejoices over the younger one (Jesus) coming into the world to do a brand-new thing. Oh, that we might do the same thing, that we would prepare the way for those that come after us. We should welcome, embrace, and bless the generations that come after us. This is the Jesus way. This is Advent.

At Christmas, through the surprising responses of John and Elizabeth, we realize God is revealing something new and different, something that offers us all great joy found in the hope of greater things than anything we've seen or experienced before, even if we're not there to see it in its fullness!

Questions for Reflection

Have you ever felt like an outcast or feel like you don't fit in?

How do you handle those perceived as "misfits" in your life? Who are they? Why don't they fit in?

Where do you see yourself in Mary, Elizabeth or Robert L. May's story?

Are you making room—like John and Elizabeth do and as Mary does for Jesus—for the One who is coming after us? If so, how? If not, what might help you open up and let Christ in?

The Surprising Closed Door at Christmas

About that time Caesar Augustus ordered a census to be taken throughout the Empire. This was the first census when Quirinius was governor of Syria. Everyone had to travel to his own ancestral hometown to be accounted for. So Joseph went from the Galilean town of Nazareth up to Bethlehem in Judah, David's town, for the census. As a descendant of David, he had to go there. He went with Mary, his fiancée, who was pregnant. While they were there, the time came for her to give birth. She gave birth to a son, her firstborn. She wrapped him in a blanket and laid him in a manger because there was no room in the hostel (in the inn).

Luke 2:1-7 (MSG)

As we approach Christmas, we draw near to Bethlehem and the beloved Lukan account of the birth of Jesus. We find ourselves in the anticipated and familiar story of Jesus involving the living nativity with all the familiar characters and plot lines. However, upon deeper inspection, I contend all the details don't seem to work as we've grown accustomed to imagining.

One of the things we discover upon reading Luke's account in depth is that Mary and Joseph weren't kicked

69

out of a hotel or an inn with no vacancy. Instead of lying in a stable outside a full-service hotel or hostel, Mary and Joseph are given the ground level, rear portion of an ancestral family home where typically the animals were fed, protected, and housed in the winter. This is where they deliver the holy infant, not because there wasn't any room in the overbooked hotel, but rather because there is no room in the family's "guest room."

Kataluma is the ancient Greek word Luke uses to describe the unavailable space in his birth narrative, and *kataluma* points to an upper-level room found in the most typical Palestinian home. This word is used again in Luke 22 to describe the Upper Room, the meeting place and site of the Last Supper where Jesus shared his body and blood with his disciples before departing them. This was the overcrowded space in the Christmas story. Mary and Joseph had to go to and deliver their child in a feeding trough surrounded by animals because there wasn't any room in their family's house.

I find it fascinating that there was never any mention of an innkeeper—meaning there was no well-intentioned innkeeper closing the door on them in their greatest hour of need. That might be a good thing if you're having trouble filling roles in a children's Christmas pageant. However, what this implies is that somebody else played that role in the original story. And given that Joseph and Mary were returning home to be with family on account of the global census, that "somebody" was a part of their family. Somebody they knew, someone in their family, closed the door on them as they were seeking refuge. Somebody they knew was responsible for sending them to deliver their child in a manger. How does that change things for you?

In Ancient Greek, the word *pandocheion* was used to describe what we call a hotel or an inn. Similarly, Luke uses this word elsewhere in the gospel as well. He uses it in Luke 10 during the parable of the Good Samaritan. You remember that story, right? Luke writes:

> *But wanting to justify himself, [the young attorney] asked Jesus, "And who is my neighbor?" Jesus replied, "A man was going down from Jerusalem to Jericho, and fell into the hands of robbers, who stripped him, beat him, and went away, leaving him half dead. Now by chance a priest was going down that road; and when he saw him, he passed by on the other side. So likewise a Levite, when he came to the place and saw him, passed by on the other side. But a Samaritan while travelling came near him; and when he saw him, he was moved with pity. He went to him and bandaged his wounds, having poured oil and wine on them. Then he put him on his own animal, brought him to an inn, and took care of him. The next day he took out two denarii, gave them to the innkeeper, and said, 'Take care of him; and when I come back, I will repay you whatever more you spend.' Which of these three, do you think, was a neighbor to the man who fell into the hands of the robbers?" He said, "The one who showed him mercy." Jesus said to him, "Go and do likewise."*

Luke 10:25-37 (NRSV)

Whereas the Good Samaritan successfully travelled and brought the beaten man, left for dead in the ditch, to an inn, Mary and Joseph traveled home to be with their family. One was welcome. One wasn't. The innkeeper made way for the man in the ditch. Joseph's family didn't make room for the newest addition to their family. The innkeeper opened the door for the beaten man. Joseph's own family closed the door on Christmas.

How does this change your understanding of the Christmas story?

What would a children's pageant look like if this were the dominant storyline?

Why do you think Joseph's family was unwilling to make room for Mary and Joseph in their guest room?

There are hundreds of reasons why this could have happened. Perhaps the family guest room was packed with other family members who were already soundly sleeping. *(Never mind that Mary was about to deliver a child after journeying seventy miles!)* In that case, the downstairs, back-of-the-house stable might have been the best the family had to offer.

It could have been that the questionable nature of Mary's pregnancy still hadn't settled in for the in-laws. Perhaps Joseph's family was still ashamed, hurt, or afraid of what would become of them because of this child. In that case, putting them in the stable with the animals might have been the best place to hide them to protect them from punishment.

Maybe Joseph's family members were all kosher Jews who knew that the whole house would become unclean if a woman gave birth inside it. In that case, putting them outside with the animals was the right and faithful thing to do. Or perhaps Joseph's family had simply rejected him/them altogether.

Which of these hypothetical scenarios or reasons seem most plausible to you?

Regardless of your answer, one thing remains: there was no room for them. The first door Jesus ever encountered in Bethlehem was surprisingly shut, closed by the ones who, by all accounts, should have been the first to open the door.

It is a challenging story to read in this way. This could be your story. Perhaps you're processing through closed doors between you and your loved ones this season. If you are, I want you to know that Jesus is with you. He's been there. In that way, the Christmas story is *your* story too. I assure you, there's no place we can go that Jesus hasn't first gone for us. In this way, Christmas should remind you that you are never alone; God is with you.

This story is also about our relationship with Jesus and the doors that we've closed on God or that have been shut in our life. When you stop to think about your life, it's easy to begin seeing the doors that have closed all around us throughout our lifetime, but sometimes it is harder to see where we have been the ones actively closing doors. In that way, this Christmas story could also be a story about you, too—meaning perhaps you have been in the place of Joseph's family, closing doors on those you love.

The good news, regardless of where you are in the story, is that the Christmas story doesn't end with a closed door. It continues as God presses on through Joseph and Mary.

God refuses to honor the doors we close all around our lives. Christmas is the story about an intrusive God who is determined, at all costs, to be Emmanuel, God with us. Thomas Merton writes:

> "Into this world, this demented inn, in which there is absolutely no room for Him at all, Christ has come uninvited...it is not the last gasp of exhausted possibilities, but the first taste of all that is beyond conceiving."[12]

The story of Christmas is the surprising announcement of God, who never stops searching

---

[12]   https://discipleswalk.org/into-this-world-thomas-merton/.

for people like Mary and Joseph to bring about God's everlasting light, new life, peace, hope, and love. The God we meet at the manger is the God who never stops knocking on and pressing through the closed doors of our lives. God's love is relentless in this way.

You see this so clearly in Bethlehem at Christmas, but God confirms this in Revelation. The New Testament ends in Revelation as the Risen Christ says:

> *Look! I'm standing at the door knocking. If any of you hear my voice, open the door, I will come in to be with them and will have dinner with them and they will have dinner with me.*
>
> **Revelation 3:20 (NRSV)**

The relentless love of God will never stop knocking on closed doors, no matter how many times we shut them. Jesus says, "I will be with you always, even to the end of the age" (Matthew 28:20 NKJV)!

Christmas is a time to tear all our barriers down. None of us wants to acknowledge the space in our souls, the emptiness in our hearts, the hollowness in our compassion, or the shallowness of our hopes. We don't like to see or even think of the doors we've closed, but on Christmas Eve, these doors are brought into plain view through Luke's account of Christmas.

For the first-century Galileans who witnessed Jesus' public ministry, it was easy to open their lives to Christ during his public ministry. People were open to Jesus' power and presence. They followed Jesus wherever he went, which was especially true for the nonreligious and nominally religious people. For most of them, Jesus' life, his mission, love, and presence were magnetic.

Matthew mentions the crowds that followed Jesus more than any of the gospel writers, but Luke, Mark, and John speak of the crowds as well. The crowds around Jesus were explicitly mentioned thirty-four times by name in the gospels. In addition to those mentions, it's important to remember that most of Jesus' words, the miracles he performed, the healings, and teachings all happened in front of crowds or as crowds pressed in around him. This was especially true in Capernaum, Jesus' home base during his earthly ministry.

It was in Capernaum where the four friends lowered a paralytic, their fifth friend, down through a hole in the thatch of the roof simply to get to Jesus. The reason they had to go to such lengths was because the crowds of people were blocking every other entry into the house.

It was in Capernaum where Jesus was walking through the crowds, carving his way home, only to be interrupted by Jairus, the leader of the synagogue. Jairus' daughter was near death, and he longed for Jesus to do something about it. Jairus wanted Jesus to heal her. So, upon agreeing to do what he could, Jesus started walking with Jairus: *"And a large crowd followed him and pressed in on him"* (Mark 5:24 NRSV).

There's urgency in this scene. There's movement in this scene. The crowds were pressing in all around Jesus, and Jesus was in his vintage "whatever it takes" form. As Jairus and Jesus approached the house, Mark suddenly shifts our attention to an unseen woman lying motionless on the ground. She's depleted and discouraged due to a decade's worth of hemorrhaging. She's stuck in the middle of the crowd.

There was a woman who had been suffering from hemorrhages for twelve years. She had endured much under many physicians, and had spent all that she had; and she was no better, but rather grew worse. She had heard about Jesus, and came up behind him in the crowd and touched his cloak, for she said, "If I but touch his clothes, I will be made well."
Mark 5:25-28 (NRSV)

As Jesus and this crowd walked past her—or perhaps over her—she began to stir. She mustered enough strength to reach out her arm between the crowded tangle of feet and ankles, hoping to touch Jesus. I think about this scene, and I think, *What strength she had! What kind of desperation must she have possessed to compel her to move amongst the masses toward Jesus?*

Jesus stopped to heal this woman. And then he continues on to heal Jairus' daughter. Immediately after that, Mark describes how everybody is overcome with amazement. Jesus went on to spend the next three years of his life preaching to the masses on the mounts and in the plains, feeding thousands, healing crowds, binding up the broken, loving the unlovable, visiting the lonely, serving the least, finding the lost and, all the while, inviting people to follow him. And they did. They couldn't help themselves. Nobody could resist Jesus. Jesus' life and love, his power and presence were so magnetic. There were no barriers. Their lives, the hearts, and minds of the masses were all open to Jesus.

What happened to us?

When did we stop freely and willingly opening our lives to Jesus?

When did things change?

Things changed well before us. They first changed at the crucifixion. That was the most notable moment in history when everything went dark, and it happened to those same first-century Galileans. The crucifixion marks the first time when the people who really knew Jesus closed the door on him. At the crucifixion, Jesus' closest friends, his disciples, wiped clean their experience of and their connection to him altogether. The very same people that Jesus fed, healed, loved, and cared for all abandoned him in that moment. The crucifixion was the first moment in history when everybody disappeared. All his followers fell away. They slammed the door shut.

But God refuses to honor the doors we close—and we don't simply see this at Christmas; we also see it at Easter. This is the hope found in the Resurrection. The worst thing is never the last thing. Christmas and Easter are tied together in this way.

On Easter, we celebrate the Resurrection, where Jesus declares once again that he is with us always. The Resurrection confirms what we celebrate at Christmas: there's nothing we'll ever face that Jesus hasn't faced first. Easter declares that God's life triumphs over death, the light of Christ defeats the darkness, the hope of the world replaces our despair, and most importantly, God's love conquers hate. Easter, like Christmas, changes everything.

We no longer have to be afraid; we should no longer worry or weep or do any of those human things. We should no longer close any doors. We should rejoice, sing "Hallelujah," and live differently with the confidence of the children of God! Every Sunday after Easter should be treated as a Resurrection Day, a day when we gather together to rejoice and resolve to live differently. And I suppose most of us do live differently, at least for a little bit—until we don't, and then we start closing doors again. This is our rhythm. And we aren't alone; this was the disciples' rhythm as well.

After Easter, for the next forty days, Jesus appeared before the disciples, trying to convince them to open up to his surprising power and presence once again. And for forty days, the disciples were reluctant, confused, afraid, and often hiding behind closed doors.

Sometimes, I think we, the American church, are at a point not too far removed from this reality right now. We're getting more and more prone to closing the door on Jesus—and there are so many empty churches.

A recent Pew Research study shares that the percentage of U.S. adults who identify as Christian has dropped from 77 percent to 65 percent. There has been a 12-point decline in self-professed faithfulness among American adults of every generation over the past decade. The flip side of this statistic is that there has been an increase in the percentage of people claiming to be religiously unaffiliated. Whereas 17 percent of the population called themselves "nothing in particular" ten years ago, over 26 percent say the same thing today. That's a significant increase.

When it comes to the emerging generations, these statistics are only further exaggerated. Nearly 40 percent of the emerging generations call themselves "nothing in particular," and less than half claim Christianity—which means "following Jesus" has lost its luster. Jesus, the church, and the living body of Christ have become resistible. Half of the younger generations are choosing to follow "nothing in particular" over Jesus.[13] We are closing the door again.

The good news is that God doesn't stop at closed doors. The story of Christmas and the story of Easter both share the surprising announcement of God, who never stops coming down to search for people like Mary and Joseph, for people like the twelve disciples, or for people like you and me. The God we meet at the manger is the same God we meet at Easter, and both Christmas and Easter work together and offer us a full picture of the God of the Universe who never stops pursuing us, knocking on the closed doors of our lives relentlessly longing to enter in.

God finally enters back into the disciples' lives fifty days after the first Easter. The disciples were hiding behind locked doors for fear of what might become of them. They were back in the *kataluma,* the very same place that had been closed off to Jesus in Bethlehem. On Pentecost, the Holy Spirit finally breaks through (in John's gospel, Jesus simply walks through the closed door and breathes on his disciples). The Holy Spirit, the surprising power and presence of God, fills the disciples and inspires them and ultimately catapults them out into the world, breaking them free from all the closed doors that had been holding them back.

---

[13]   https://www.pewresearch.org/religion/2019/10/17/in-u-s-decline-of-christianity-continues-at-rapid-pace/.

The Holy Spirit is like dynamite in our lives. The Holy Spirit is a catalyst that inspires bold action and makes it possible for us to reflect the light and love of Jesus to the world around us. This is what happened to Peter, despite the fact that he had denied Jesus three times. By the power of the Holy Spirit, Peter was empowered to preach the good news with great joy to the whole world just a stone's throw from where he was afraid to even acknowledge knowing Jesus in a conversation. The other disciples experienced this empowerment, too, as they went out speaking and sharing the love of Christ with anyone who had ears to hear in languages they could understand. It also happened with Mary, Elizabeth, Joseph, Zechariah, Simeon, and so many of the Christmas characters who were open to receiving the surprising promise and power of God. This is *our* story too.

Just as each of these figures was thrust outside their comfort zones into the world, God meets us too. The disciples began building Christian communities defined by their worship, their prayer, and their care for those in need, and people were drawn to them. They were amazed and astonished by what they saw and heard coming out of these communities. It was so different, so visible. By the power of the Holy Spirit, they were witnesses. And they were drawing people to the life-changing power and presence of God. This is what Christ calls us to do as well, but it all starts with the surprising, closed door of Christmas in Bethlehem.

The relentless love of God never stops knocking on the closed doors of this world. Jesus' love never ends. It doesn't stop. In the *kataluma*, with his family and friends, Jesus says:

> *I give you a new commandment, that you love one another. Just as I have loved you, you also should love one another. By this everyone will know that you are my disciples, if you have love for one another.*
>
> **John 13:34-35 (NRSV)**

Jesus commands us to love others the way he first loved us. He doesn't command us to love one another the way we first loved him, but the way he first loved us.

What does that love look like?

It looks like something that never quits. It is persistent, sacrificial, always there, meeting us wherever we are, no matter how hard things may seem. Jesus' love is a love that always shows up, no questions asked. Jesus' love opens the door to everybody always. *"Love like this,"* he says. *"By this people will know that you are my disciples."* This command is the ethical standard for every Christ-follower. To love like Jesus is our calling.

Living and loving like Christ is the church's task. It's our responsibility—not just at Christmas and Easter, but every day.

The Apostle Paul urges the earliest Christian communities to love one another. He doesn't call them to belief or to faith but rather to love. This is the mark of a true Christian. Paul, writing to the Colossian church, says:

> *Therefore, as God's choice, holy and loved, put on compassion, kindness, humility, gentleness, and patience. Be tolerant with each other and, if someone has a complaint against anyone, forgive each other. As the Lord forgave you, so also forgive each other. And over all these things put on love, which is the perfect bond of unity.*
>
> **Colossians 3:12-14 (NRSV)**

Paul suggests that we live with mercy—compassion and kindness. He urges us to humility, gentleness, and patience. We should be seen as people who live and love like this, like Jesus, who never conformed to the world, but was transformed by a love and unwavering devotion to us, even when we didn't deserve it.

Paul says:

> *Let love be genuine; hate what is evil, hold fast to what is good; love one another with mutual affection; outdo one another in showing honor. Rejoice with those who rejoice, weep with those who weep. Live in harmony with one another; do not be haughty, but associate with the lowly; do not claim to be wiser than you are. Do not repay anyone evil for evil, but take thought for what is noble in the sight of all. If it is possible, so far as it depends on you, live peaceably with all...do not be overcome by evil, but overcome evil with good.*
>
> **Romans 12:9-21, selected verses (NRSV)**

Love like this. By your love for one another. When you live and love like Jesus, this is how others will come to know God. When you love others, serve others, and care for others, this is how people will come to know the irresistible power of Jesus.

Andy Stanley shares:

> *Post-churched and de-churched folks find even the best churches perfectly resistible. Why? They aren't church people. It's not what they do. In many cases it's not what they do anymore. It's not that they don't know what church is. Just the opposite. They know just enough about church to know it's not for them. Creating better churches won't change that. Making better churches isn't the answer. The answer is to return to a resurrection centered, new covenant, love one another version of our faith. The version of our faith that got things kicked off to begin with. Unchurched people may not be interested in church, but they certainly want to be one-anothered. Especially when things aren't going well.*[14]

That's what Christmas is all about. It's not about a night we go to church, have a moment, and then return to our daily living behind the closed doors of our comfortable spaces. It's about realizing that God loves us so much that he presses past whatever door we might close to prove God's love for us. There is no place God won't go, nothing God won't do to show God's love.

At Christmas, our realities change as a baby is born,

---

[14] Andy Stanley, *Irresistible: Reclaiming the New that Jesus Unleashed for the World* (Zondervan, 2018).

despite the circumstances, in a manger surrounded by animals, under the cover of night as only the silent stars go by. God chooses, at all costs, to be with us by becoming like us so we might know that we are never alone and that God longs for us to love one another in the same way so that everybody might come to know God's love for them.

The church isn't something static. It's not some big place to go to. Christmas, in the same way, isn't a point in time. It's something that shapes our reality in a brand-new way. It's a way of living with renewed confidence, knowing that God is with us, and because God is with us, we have nothing to fear; we simply have reason to rejoice. And the byproduct of that joy is love, something we're called to go and do—like every day. The church, the living body of Christ, a collection of people called to model the irresistible life and love of Jesus, to live a life of love so markedly different and unwavering that it has the power to draw people to it no matter how down, far away, in the pit they may feel or may have been in.

By your love for one another, when you live and love like me, this is how others will come to know me, says Jesus.

Can you remember or think of someone who has shared the love of Christ with you?

Is there someone in your life that God might be calling you to share the love of Christ with?

I've learned that you can't quickly forget people who have demonstrated Christ-like love in your life. When thinking about my own experience and someone who has modeled this kind of love in my life over the past several years, I think of a woman named Judi. Judi was a leader at a local recovery ministry in Kansas City. She was a member of my church, and for more than ten years, she was someone I considered to be a dear friend. I walked with her through everything imaginable. I walked beside her and witnessed her as she answered phone calls, hosted interviews, and met with people at the end of their ropes, at rock bottom. In almost every instant, Judi managed to find a way to say, "We'll make a space for you. Just come home." She opened the door.

I remember speaking with Judi the week she was diagnosed with stage four pancreatic and liver cancer. While we sat together, I asked her, "Judi, what has been the most impactful thing that has happened to you over these last four weeks living with this diagnosis and unexpected reality?" Judi shared how she was completely and utterly overwhelmed by the amount of love she had received from the other leaders at her organization. Judi shared how, while she was stuck at the hospital, they renovated her house. "They put brand-new beds on the first floor, remodeled the bathroom, and made a space for me to come back home! They rearranged my whole house while finding the time to continue working and sleeping beside me at the hospital during my stay. I never experienced a love so unrelenting."

Judi shared how they continued to amaze her since she'd been back home. "They have hosted surprise award presentations. They organized a Super Bowl watch party. They put together a recovery ministry version of a Super Bowl celebration parade all for me." Judi said she always knew of their love, but seeing sacrificial love in action in life's darkest moments was life-changing for her. She had seen Christ in and through her dear friends, and because of that, she knew unequivocally that God was with her. There were no more closed doors, just Emmanuel.

This is the kind of love God longs for us to share. This is a love that doesn't quit.

Jesus longs for us to live and love this way—always. *By this, people will know that you are mine.* This kind of life begins at Christmas as the light of Christ pierces the darkness, and it continues as we carry that same light out into the world.

Jesus reminds his disciples in the Sermon on the Mount: *"In the same way, let your light shine before others, so that they may see your good works and give glory to your Father in heaven"* (Matthew 5:16 NRSV).

Questions for Reflection

Where in your life are you not letting Jesus in? Where are you throwing up a "No Vacancy" sign in your life of faith?

Where are you closing the door on the world around you on loving others the way that Jesus loves us?

How might you open the doors you've closed on others in the past—maybe even family—and open your life to Christ?

To love like Jesus is our calling. Does this kind of love define your life and how you seek to live it?

Where have you experienced this kind of love? Who in your life has modeled or shared the love of Christ with you? Take a moment to write down the names of people in your life who have modeled the love of Christ for you. And then write down the names of people who God might be calling you to love this Christmas.

Covid, Christmas, and Life's Unwanted Journeys

I remember the feeling like it was yesterday, even though it was over three years ago now. You probably do too. I'm talking about COVID. At first, we started hearing stories of outbreaks and quarantines related to a novel virus somewhere in a foreign place called Wuhan. A little time passed, and we began seeing pictures of people wearing masks in faraway places. Then cruise ships were docked, then there were the reports of people dying, and that's when the daily news of individual cases began surfacing here in the States. From that point forward, things escalated quickly, and our understanding of time has been obscured permanently.

For me, COVID became real in March of 2020 at about the time when the Big 12 Men's Basketball Tournament canceled all of their games. That was a defining moment—not because I'm a basketball fan but because that's typically when downtown Kansas City comes back to life after what always feels like a long winter in the Midwest. The arena doors were closed, and just a few days after that, we, as a church, closed ours as well. We didn't stop worshiping. We simply pivoted—remember that word—we began focusing on our ministry online and on television. Never in my life could I have imagined a time when the church wasn't meeting in person. To be honest, I couldn't imagine much of what happened over those months. And I feel like we've been on this crazy journey ever since—a journey that none of us wanted.

For my wife, Wendy, and I, COVID came during a particularly unique season in our life. During this time, we were expecting our second child. We had a baby girl on the way, and wouldn't you guess it, she was ready to meet the world the day before Kansas City entered its very first stay-at-home order. Thankfully, I was able to be with Wendy in the labor and delivery room as long as I had a mask on. Unfortunately, Wendy had to be masked as well, which wasn't very much fun given the work she had ahead of her. However, that wasn't the hard part—Wendy might disagree—but what was hard was realizing how different our daughter Poppy's life would be. Her experience of the world was going to be very different than what we had hoped for her. The first several months of Poppy's life were spent in isolation, separated from family, friends, neighbors, visits, hugs, and all the familiar warmth and facial expressions newborns and their families generally expect. This, too, was a journey we didn't want or welcome. In fact, over three years later, most people in our life still haven't met Poppy. And if they did, they do a doubletake because she is now a toddler. For us, her growth marks the amount of time that has passed since we began this crazy journey together.

I imagine you all have your own experience of unwanted journeys—and I'm not simply talking about COVID. My guess is you've been through unwanted journeys of grief. Maybe you've lost a loved one, a patient, a family member, or a friend. Or maybe you've walked the unexpected and unwanted journey of unemployment and financial insecurity. Maybe you've lost your job, or you're afraid of losing your job. Of course, there are all sorts of unexpected and unwanted journeys marked by fear, uncertainty about the future, loneliness, depression, addiction, isolation, and confusion.

And now, with Mary in the ninth month of her pregnancy, she and Joseph—who are somehow managing to keep it all together—get a visit from some Roman soldiers announcing a global census and that every Jewish family must return to the husband's hometown to be counted; no exceptions. The beginning of the birth of Jesus occurs as Mary and Joseph are quite literally facing an unwanted, seventy-plus-mile, nine-day journey by foot from Nazareth to Bethlehem without any notice. This is Advent. This is Christmas. Have yourself a merry little Christmas, Mary! Can you imagine that?

Mary and Joseph are just days away from the birth of their first child and facing a return trip to Bethlehem.

This was an unwanted journey if ever there was one.
What's interesting about this particular journey is
that we can absolutely know they didn't want to go to
Bethlehem because they had a chance to make the same
exact trip four months earlier (when Mary was much less
pregnant), and they chose not to go. If they didn't want to
go then, they absolutely didn't want to go now.

Have you ever wondered about what happened over
the course of those four months?

One of my favorite aspects of the Christmas story is
trying to ascertain what happened in the four months
between the time Mary visited Elizabeth and the journey
Mary and Joseph took from Nazareth to Bethlehem.
There are about four months of unaccounted-for time
between those two events. What we know is, after
spending three months with Elizabeth in Ein Karem,
Mary returns to Nazareth about four months into her
pregnancy. While Mary is back, we also know that God
meets Joseph in a dream. God confirms for Joseph that
Mary is indeed carrying God's son, which prompts
Joseph to accelerate plans for what most would refer to
as a "rushed" wedding. Matthew writes:

> [Joseph] did as the angel of the Lord commanded him; he
> took her as his wife, but had no marital relations with
> her until she had borne a son; and he named him Jesus.
>
> **Matthew 1:24-25 (NRSV)**

By the time they were wed, Mary was about five months pregnant, which means they had four months together as husband and wife before delivering the baby. After being wed, it was customary for bridal couples to live with the parents of the groom. If they were following custom, what Mary and Joseph should have done was move to Bethlehem after their wedding—but they didn't. They chose to stay put in Nazareth after the wedding. And I don't blame them. Do you? They only had four months before the baby was to be born, and they had just come through a crazy season. They needed a break. They deserved a break. Nazareth gave them that break. Staying in Nazareth, Mary and Joseph were surrounded and supported by Mary's family and friends. Things were predictable and comfortable there. Joseph could find work there, and most importantly, it didn't require any unnecessary travel, which was ideal.

Sometimes, when I think of Mary and Joseph's time in Nazareth, I imagine a young couple trying to come into their own, managing their new life together, and figuring out new rhythms of cohabitation, all while nesting in anticipation of their first child. And just when they manage to catch their breath, that's when the wheels fall off. I imagine two Roman soldiers came knocking on the door with breaking news about what I might consider to be like the first-century version of COVID. These soldiers didn't declare a global pandemic. Instead, they announced a mandatory global census.

> *A decree went out from Emperor Augustus that all the world should be registered. This was the first registration and was taken while Quirinius was governor of Syria.*
>
> **Luke 2:1 (NRSV)**

I can imagine the kinds of questions that raced through their minds. How did they feel? What did their prayers sound like? God, how could you? You can't be serious! You came and asked us to raise this child, and now this? Why?

This would have been hard—like really hard. This nine-day, seventy-plus-mile journey by foot from Nazareth to Bethlehem in the ninth month of Mary's pregnancy wasn't the same as having mask mandates reinstated or stay-at-home orders enforced, but it was close, right?

No, not at all! Try to remember how you felt about COVID setbacks and restrictions and multiply that by a million. What Mary and Joseph were facing was far worse. Mary was nine months pregnant, she was fourteen, and they had to walk seventy miles through the mountains. It was awful—and this was Christmas. It wasn't all merry and bright. This was an unwanted journey.

When we read and remember this ancient story, we are forced to acknowledge that life is sometimes hard. There are seasons when we find ourselves stuck facing unwanted journeys. Our time during the COVID crisis is proof of that for us. We didn't want that journey. But the Christmas story reminds us that we aren't alone in these unwanted journeys, and these unwanted journeys don't last forever.

The good news is that the Christmas story doesn't end with a knock on the door in Nazareth. It ends with a baby born in Bethlehem in the light of the moon. And this isn't just any baby. The baby born in Bethlehem is Jesus, Emmanuel, God with us, in the flesh. At Christmas, the God of the Universe chooses to enter our reality at our darkest hour, at the tail end of a nine-day, seventy-plus-mile journey by foot in the ninth month of pregnancy, swollen ankles and all.

God chooses to meet us on that journey. And God doesn't meet us in a palace but in a stable, lying in a feeding trough, surrounded by animals and shepherds under the cover of night. The God of the Universe meets us and is with us at our lowest, darkest moments, in the messiness of our most unwanted journeys. *This is the good news of great joy we experience at Christmas.*

This is how much God loves us. God's faithfulness has no bounds. At Christmas, we find surprising hope knowing that there isn't any journey we could ever go on where God won't be with us. Jesus is Emmanuel, God with us, not just sometimes but all the time. Nothing can separate us from God's love!

Do you believe this? Sometimes it's hard to believe and accept.

I imagine there were moments on the journey from Nazareth to Bethlehem when Mary and Joseph felt abandoned, exhausted, and scared, and moments where they wondered if they were going to make it. In those moments, I imagine the Christ child kicking in Mary's womb, causing Mary to flinch and Joseph to wrap his arms around his bride, all the while drawing them closer to each other and closer to God. I also believe the love of this child fueled them, the presence of God with them.

A few years back, I visited Israel with a big group of people. It just so happened that several people within that group had recently been on unwanted journeys of grief, having lost loved ones, spouses, and even children. At one of our stops, we got out of the buses and spent intentional time walking through the rugged terrain of the Judean wilderness near a route that Mary and Joseph could have traveled on their journey. The Judean wilderness is best described as barren and full of rocky mountainous terrain. It is dry and devoid of any signs of life.

Standing in the wilderness, it is easy to feel alone against the vastness of such rugged and unforgiving terrain. I like to stop at one particular spot amid the barrenness because it allows everybody who visits the Holy Land an opportunity to be still, to pause, and just breathe. I invite people to take half an hour or so simply to pray, journal, read scripture, and connect with God. So, people fan out across the terrain, and things get really quiet.

One of the people on this trip had lost her spouse earlier that year. She was on an unwanted journey, to say the least. So, when the time came, she ventured away from the crowd, sat down, and started to pray. I remember her sharing how she had been vacillating between praying and crying, but in that quiet time of reflection, something happened. She said, "It was the weirdest thing. It was like I could hear running water— like a river or something." She said, "I couldn't see it, but I could hear it. It was there. It was definitely there." And she said it reminded her of Psalm 23: *Even though I walk through the darkest valley, I fear no evil; for you are with me; your rod and your staff—they comfort me* (Psalm 23:4 NRSV). At her darkest hour, she knew she wasn't alone. She heard the living water and felt that God was with her, and she experienced God's peace. This unwanted journey didn't define her anymore. Jesus did. Emmanuel, God, was with her, and that gave her strength to carry on. It fueled her.

By the way, she did actually hear running water. The

mountains are so beautiful in the Judean wilderness because they've been cut by living (or moving) water throughout the ages. At the base of these steep and jagged peaks are riverbeds that continue to flow and fill up with living water, and those waters have served and soothed generations of weary travelers, reminding them that God is with us always.

This is the Christmas story in miniature. Christmas reveals the relentless love God has for us in our daily journeys. And that love is most certainly a love that meets us in the middle of our messes, at the end of our journeys in the form of a baby, or a friend, or through the sound of rushing water, as a way of reminding us that God is making all things new again. God reserves God's best work for the most unwanted moments in our lives. I think about the countless stories of scripture where God doesn't leave or forsake us but instead stands with us in the middle of the storm or the fire or the pits of life. I think about Joseph, who was sold into slavery by his brothers, or Shadrach, Meshach, and Abednego, who were tossed into a fiery furnace. In the same way, God's faithfulness and love met and redeemed David, Ruth, and every generation leading to Mary and Joseph, in the messiness of their life together, at the darkest hours of their journey and redeemed them. This is the power of God's love for us.

The prophet Isaiah speaks of God's love saying:

*Do not fear, for I have redeemed you; I have called
you by name, you are mine. When you pass through
the waters, I will be with you; and through the rivers,
they shall not overwhelm you; when you walk through
fire you shall not be burned, and the flame shall not
consume you. For I am the Lord your God, the Holy
One of Israel, your Savior.*

Isaiah 43:1-3 (NRSV)

God loves us, chases after us, longs to be with us no
matter what we might be facing, and gives us Jesus,
the fullest expression of God's love in the flesh for our
eyes to see. However, we don't see him until our darkest
hour. The light of Christmas enters in under the cover
of night to remind us that nothing can separate us from
the light and love of Jesus. The light of Christ pierces the
darkness. John writes:

*What has come into being in him was life, and the
life was the light of all people. The light shines in the
darkness, and the darkness did not overcome it...*

*The true light, which enlightens everyone, was coming
into the world.*

John 1:4-5, 9 (NRSV)

The true light, which enlightens everyone, is coming
into the world. That light shines in the darkness, and the
darkness cannot overcome it. This is exactly what we
need. It's what we long for, especially considering the life
seasons we experience and will continue to endure.

101

Jesus is the light of the world. He pierces our darkest hours with his light and life, and he wants us to do the same thing. Throughout his earthly ministry, Jesus called his disciples time and time again to do what he did. He leads them and inspires them to love others like he loved, to shine with the light of Christ. In his Sermon on the Mount, Jesus invites us to "let your light shine before others, that they may see your good deeds and glorify your Father in heaven" (Matthew 5:16 NIV). Jesus knew that people wandering in darkness were in need of a great light, and he longs for us to share so others are drawn to the light.

In the coming days and months, my guess is that you'll have struggles, but you'll also hear of others who are traveling on unwanted journeys, walking in darkness, looking for the light, and longing for hope. My prayer is that you might become like stars for them, that you'll shine with the light of Christ and lead people to Bethlehem, to candlelight Christmas Eve, and a return to the surprising power and presence of God at Christmas.

Light the way, invite people, shine like stars, and embody the light of Christ, God with us for the world around you as we seek to return to Bethlehem every day of our life together.

Questions for Reflection

What sustains you or fuels you when you're in the darkness?

How might you be a beacon of light to those experiencing darkness? Describe specific ways you can share your light and the love of Jesus with others.

Unexpected Journeys
Searching for Something

*In the time of King Herod, after Jesus was born in
Bethlehem of Judea, wise men from the East came to
Jerusalem, asking, "Where is the child who has been
born king of the Jews? For we observed his star at its
rising, and have come to pay him homage." When King
Herod heard this, he was frightened, and all Jerusalem
with him; and calling together all the chief priests and
scribes of the people, he inquired of them where the
Messiah was to be born. They told him, "In Bethlehem of
Judea; for so it has been written by the prophet:*

*"And you, Bethlehem, in the land of Judah,
are by no means least among the rulers of Judah;
for from you shall come a ruler
who is to shepherd my people Israel."*

*Then Herod secretly called for the wise men and learned
from them the exact time when the star had appeared.
Then he sent them to Bethlehem, saying, "Go and
search diligently for the child; and when you have found
him, bring me word so that I may also go and pay
him homage." When they had heard the king, they set
out; and there, ahead of them, went the star that they
had seen at its rising, until it stopped over the place
where the child was. When they saw that the star had
stopped, they were overwhelmed with joy. On entering*

*the house, they saw the child with Mary his mother; and
they knelt down and paid him homage. Then, opening
their treasure-chests, they offered him gifts of gold,
frankincense, and myrrh. And having been warned in
a dream not to return to Herod, they left for their own
country by another road.*

Matthew 2:1-12 (NRSV)

As we close this five-week Advent study, it is
important to conclude with the three kings. After all,
"We Three Kings" is one of my favorite Christmas
hymns. (We began with singing, so it is only fitting that
we end with it as well!)

Even though they're only given twelve lines of face
time in scripture, everyone seems to know and love the
story of the three kings. We sing songs about the three
kings; we covet the gifts they bear; and if given the
opportunity, each of us would secretly dress up like one
of these kings.

When we launched Resurrection Downtown in
2009 (an urban church plant in the heart of downtown
Kansas City), we did so under the assumption that
there wouldn't be any children. It was a city center,
and there weren't many spaces for children in the lofts
and high rises. There was, however, an abundance of
young entrepreneurs and established empty nesters. As
it turned out, it didn't matter what the demographics
of the city were; we actually ended up having loads of

kids visiting our new church. So, like every new church start, we scrambled to make space for them, and come Christmastime, we worked frantically to find a Sunday to feature our kids. Let the children lead the way! So, we decided to have our very first "Downtown Children's Christmas Pageant." Can I tell you, these kids were fighting over their roles. They weren't fighting over the roles of Mary or Joseph or even the angels. They were all about the kings! They were vying to be Balthasar, Caspar, and Melchior! For the life of me, I couldn't figure out why.

Who were these kings?

Where were they from? Persia? Babylon? China?

Were they even kings? Or were they astrologers? Wise men?

And what about these gifts of gold, frankincense, and myrrh? What were those? And were they intentional?

Why did every kid want to be one?

In Chapter 60 of Isaiah, the prophet writes:

> *Nations shall come to your light, and kings to the*
> *brightness of your dawn. Lift up your eyes and*
> *look around; they all gather together...they come*
> *to you; the wealth of the nations shall come to you.*
> *A multitude of camels shall cover you, the young*
> *camels of Midian and Ephah; all those from Sheba*
> *shall come. They shall bring gold and frankincense*
> *and shall proclaim the praise of the Lord.*
>
> **Isaiah 60, selected verses (NRSV)**

In the days that followed the arrival of the Coming
One, Isaiah says that kings and nations will come to
Israel. They'll gather around you, and wealth will
abound! Isaiah even goes so far as to say that a multitude
of camels will show up on the day the Messiah comes.
And then together, the camels, nations, and kings will all
praise God and give the children of Israel glory.

Isaiah's prophecy leaves all the people of Israel—and
us—expecting a royal welcome from the nations upon
Christ's birth. It's from this prophecy that we get the
song "We Three Kings of Orient Are." And it's from
this prophecy that we dream about dressing up in great
costumes, complete with blinged-out entourages, flexing
our gifts of frankincense, gold, and myrrh, riding on not
one but a multitude of camels.

As Matthew tells the story, he never mentions that
these visitors from the East were "kings." Instead,
Matthew tells us that these visitors brought Christ the

kingly gifts of gold, frankincense, and myrrh. He doesn't call them "kings." He calls them "Magi."

Matthew uses the Greek word *magoi,* which most commonly refers to "wise men," but even that's a bit vague. What made them wise? This word *magoi* is used in one other place in scripture: Acts 13.

Paul and Barnabas are commissioned to go and preach the Gospel to all the Gentiles, and on their way to Cyprus, they just so happen to meet up with two Magi (*magoi*), which in this case refers to "magicians" or "false prophets"—two things, by the way, that are very different than kings. So perhaps we should consider that these visitors from the East weren't kings at all but magicians or prophets of another god coming to see the Christ. That's one of a variety of meanings for the word *Magi.*

Magi could have referred to "Magians," or members of the Persian priestly caste or Zoroastrian priests. Magians followed the stars as a way of worshiping the one God. In this scenario, we read the story of the Magi and should envision a group of people who were following the stars in search of God. They pursued God by watching the stars as they rose and fell. Maybe these Magi were priests of another religion who met Jesus and were overjoyed when they saw where the star had stopped.

More recently, though, there's some scholarly consensus forming which says that these Magi, these wise men/magicians (or Zoroastrians), were just astrologers; they were sky readers. Just like our iPad apps, these guys could read the stars, but they could tell us more than the name of the constellations we're looking at. They could read the stars like we read the newspaper. They could look at the stars and know what was going on in this world.

Astrology was very popular in the time of Christ. It originated from "the East" and was prevalent among many Eastern religions. And since Matthew makes it clear that these wise men were prompted onto their journey by observing the stars and doesn't mention any other religions or even angels, then we can easily begin to imagine that these men were simply wise astrologers. In the end, however, I'm not sure it matters who they are. It's all about what these three figures represent.

What really matters when it comes to the Magi is recognizing that these three people were coming to see the light of Christ from a totally foreign place. They were outsiders. These wise men were not a part of the program. They weren't a part of the chosen people of Israel, and they weren't keepers of the promise. They were Gentiles, maybe even pagans.

The Magi were the biblical equivalents of whom we might today call "those people." They *were* the others, people who looked and acted differently. They were the discomforting outsiders, the oddballs, the "why are you here" kind of people as opposed to the "we're so glad you're here" types. If they were from Babylon, then they were the enemy. If they were magicians, they were the enemy. If they were false prophets, Zoroastrians, even if they were kings of other nations, they were the enemy.

The Magi were potentially following a different God, but it could have been that they weren't following God at all. What we know is that they were following things like the stars or magic or, at minimum, their own intuition, reason, and logic. And so, surprise, once again, we find in the Magi people who don't fit into the Christmas story. People didn't see this coming.

People weren't anticipating that people with different backgrounds and different religions, people who were on the outside looking in, non-religious people, or nominally religious people would be included in the Christmas story. What the presence of the Magi indicates, however, is that the story of Christmas is not simply about the consolation of Israel, but it's a story that points to the salvation of the entire world.

The story of the Magi reveals to us that the light of Christ is powerful enough to extend to and include the Gentiles. The light that has the power to poke holes in the darkness also has the power to draw in all people, and this is perhaps the most significant piece of the Christmas story. What's more is that when we see these wise men from the East fall down before God, this holy infant, offering not just their expensive gifts but the gift of their whole lives, we also get a glimpse of the future. Through the Magi, we catch a glimpse of a time that the Apostle Paul describes a time when *"every knee shall bow and every tongue confess that God is love and love has come to save us all"* (Philippians 2:10-11 NRSV)!

The surprising presence of the Magi reveals that the light of Christ and the promise of Christmas is powerful enough to draw people from afar, people who are distant and perhaps searching by any means they can to discover the promises of God's never-ending love. My guess is that you have been one of "those people" before, or maybe you are one right now, or maybe you know somebody like this. Perhaps you've been looking for something, searching for meaning, desperately longing for the light, yearning for hope, and something about Christmas this year has drawn you back to this place. Or perhaps the light of Christ has drawn you out for the very first time. I pray that you might experience the love of Christ today.

Our searching is the same as the Magi's searching. Their story is our story. Perhaps the difference is that they had a much longer and more arduous journey to get where they were going. Their journey wasn't as easy as ours. They weren't coming into a church filled with greeters at every turn, nice ushers to help them find a seat, or endless cups of the best coffee around. They weren't simply turning the pages of a book. No, their journey to Bethlehem required months' worth of travel, and their journey would ultimately lead them through Jerusalem where they would have to confront the political powers of that day. They needed to come face to face with Herod, or humanity, at its worst.

Matthew begins his account of the Magi by setting the political scene first. He writes, *"In the time of King Herod, after Jesus was born in Bethlehem of Judea, the wise men came from the East to Jerusalem"* (Matthew 2:1 NRSV).

By starting the story this way, Matthew reminds us that even though Christ had been born, this was still very much Herod's world. Herod was in charge. He was holding all the power. Herod was the king of the Jews, and all decisions flowed through him. All activity happened because of him.

There wasn't a place you could go in Jerusalem (or Bethlehem, for that matter) to escape Herod's presence. His palace mount, the Herodium, overshadowed the whole region. So Matthew says these Magi arrived on the scene in the time of Herod and not in the time of Jesus. Any journey would have had to flow through King Herod first.

As they followed the star, the wise men/magicians eventually made it all the way to Jerusalem, to the center of Israel, into the heart of Herod's kingdom, and they started asking around: *"Where is the child who has been born king of the Jews? For we observed his star at its rising, and we have come to worship him"* (Matthew 2:2 NRSV).

Within hours, the Magi were standing before Herod, and after consulting with some of his scribes, Herod gave them directions to Bethlehem, to the place where this child was, and he commanded them to go and find this child, saying: *"Go and search diligently for the child; and when you have found him, bring me word so that I may also go and pay him homage"* (Matthew 2:9 NRSV).

And so, unknowingly, the Magi agreed to share news of this child's location with Herod (who was planning to have him killed), and they set out once again. When they saw where the star stopped, they were overwhelmed with joy. They made it. The hour had finally come. They found what they were looking for. They entered the house, and once inside, they saw the child with Mary, his mother, and immediately they knelt down and paid him homage. They worshiped. They sang. They prayed. They gave him everything they had: their lives, their hearts, their hands, and their gifts, all of which carried special meaning.

One of these men gave Jesus the gift of gold, which was (and has always been) a kingly gift. Gold has historically been associated with the monarchy. Gold is a gift fit for a king, and so with this first gift, the Magi declare that this child is indeed the king. What's more, if Jesus is the king, that means that Herod cannot be. This wasn't a gift so much as it was a confession and bold proclamation.

The next wise man offered Jesus a gift of holy perfume, or frankincense. Frankincense was a fragrant substance used exclusively in the sanctuary and nowhere else. Exodus 30 describes for us that frankincense is to be used only in the holiest of places, only in worship:

> *The Lord said to Moses: Take sweet spices with pure frankincense (an equal part of each), and make an incense blended as by the perfumer, seasoned with salt, pure and holy; and you shall beat some of it into powder, and put it before the covenant in the tent of meeting where I shall meet you; it shall be for you most holy.*

Exodus 30:34-36 (NRSV)

The second gift, the gift of frankincense, acknowledges that this infant was not just king; he was indeed holy, the object of worship. He was ultimately communicating with his gift, saying, in effect, to Jesus, *You are my priest, you are my God, you are worthy of all my thanks and praise.* This second gift confesses that Jesus is God's new covenant, the promise of Christmas, the hope of the world.

Lastly, there was a third gift, the gift of myrrh. Myrrh was traditionally used in two settings. For one, it was employed in the high priest's anointing oil. Offering Christ the gift of myrrh was a way of naming him and recognizing Jesus as the "Anointed One." But myrrh was also used for something else.

In John 19, Nicodemus brought one hundred pounds of myrrh to prepare Jesus' body for burial. So this gift not only anointed the Christ child at birth, but it foreshadowed his death as well. This third gift is the gift that connects Christmas with Easter. It ties the incarnation to the cross and Resurrection. How cool is that? And these outsiders were responsible for it.

Through the giving of their gifts, these Magi reveal Christ as our Savior, as the one who will ultimately free us from slavery to sin and death, free us from the kingdom of man, free us from Herod and humanity at its worst.

These are three amazing gifts, beautiful and symbolic. They come from people who were outsiders, and yet somehow, these outsiders could see in this holy infant something remarkable, something divine, something worthy of our love, our life, and our all. This is something we all should see and acknowledge.

The story of the Magi and the story of Christmas are stories full of surprising characters, people meeting God and finding the light after spending the better part of their lives searching, wandering, and wondering in the darkness. It's a story about people searching for something and then finding it in the light of Christ, the star of Bethlehem. The Magi remind us that the Christmas story is about interconnected strangers and misfits growing in the knowledge and love of God.

116

When the Magi met Jesus, they couldn't help but fall before him in worship. They humbled themselves. They prayed. They sang. They lifted their voices in praise and thanksgiving, and then they gave God their gifts— amazing gifts, extravagant gifts. They gave everything they had. They worshiped, and then they left to go back home a different way. In other words, they were changed.

That's what typically happens when we come face to face with Christ, when we encounter the light of Christmas or meet the living God in worship. Worship should compel us like Christ. It should force us to our knees in humble adoration. It should change us. We should leave worship different than the way we walked in.

John Wesley calls this kind of change or transformation "second birth." He says when we meet God, we receive second birth, we are given a new life, and our hearts and minds are opened in such a way that enables us to walk fully into the newness of life as people whose lives are changed.

This is hard to picture—in fact, I've had trouble picturing it lately. For the Magi, it was easy. They literally met Jesus in the flesh. He was easy to see, and their encounter with Christ literally forced them to walk home differently. It is not always that easy or simple for us to see and experience Christ in the same way.

In my previous church, I spent most of my time

serving the community as a youth pastor, and if ever there was a bunch of wise guys, it was in our middle school and high school youth groups. Our student ministries were called "Awaken." Our prayer and our hope were that God would awaken us to God's hope-radiating presence and power but also that God would use us to awaken others to the life-changing promise of God's forever love.

Very early on in my time there, I met up with one of the youth I was called to shepherd. He was unruly. His head and his focus were always in the clouds. He marched to the beat of a different drum. I don't know how, but he managed to be the troublemaker, the momentum, and the one person in our youth group who didn't believe in God all at the same time. Ironically, he also loved the stars. In fact, he thought all of life's answers were found by looking to the stars. I remember talking with him about this at length.

One day, I was having a lot of trouble with this guy. He was out of control, like most high school boys, whenever there was a big crowd gathering. So, I decided to ask him if he'd be willing to help me serve communion that night in worship. Much to my surprise, he said, "Sure."

I had him hold the cup and then told him what to do. He was so nervous, but at the same time, he was so stoic in his appearance.

As people came up to him to receive communion, one by one, he would offer them the blood of Christ. And then he would watch in disbelief at how their expressions would change. His friends were weeping. Some of them were smiling. He saw others closing their eyes, saying, "Thank you, Jesus." He saw all of them continuing to worship, most often kneeling and rocking in prayer. And by the time he was done serving, he heard them all rejoicing in song.

In the days that followed this sacramental encounter in the crowd, this young man asked me what it was all about. I said, "When people come face to face with God, when people encounter Jesus in the sacraments, I actually believe they meet the one who gives us second birth, or second chances. I believe they meet the only one who has the power to change our lives for the better, and when we meet God in that way, something changes in us. We're no longer afraid, or we feel free, or we perhaps simply feel safe and loved." I'm not sure this young man understood what I was trying to explain (I'm not sure I did either), but that didn't matter because he had experienced something, and it was starting to change his life.

I baptized him later that year, and over time, he became one of our best student leaders. Never had he planned to go to college, but I'll never forget that moment when he texted me during his senior year to say, "Merry Christmas!" To which I replied saying, "Merry Christmas to you too!" And then he shared the surprising news with me that he had been accepted into college and was actually going to go. His life had totally changed.

"You are never too old to set another
goal or to dream a new dream."

C.S. Lewis

God uses Christmas and the Magi to remind us that there is a different road waiting for every one of us. These are roads filled with new goals and new dreams. These are roads of abundance and promise, roads of hope that lead toward God.

At Christmas, God becomes like us so we might become like God. In Jesus, we discover that God is with us, always, and because of that, we can be assured that all things are possible. Our lives can change, and so can our circumstances. Christ is born to give us second birth, and my prayer is that you might encounter Christ and begin living like it! Begin living as God's new creation, someone called and equipped to carry the light of Christmas into the world and bring about the kingdom of heaven here on earth just as it is in heaven. This is Christmas, this is our surprising story, and this is our life-song.

Questions for Reflection

Have you seen God this Advent? If so, where?

Where were you most surprised this season?

How will the surprises you've encountered this Advent season change how you live and love going forward?

How might God be calling you to surprise the world around you on account of your faith?

Scott Chrostek is a compelling preacher, a thoughtful interpreter of the Christian faith, and an inspiring storyteller. In Advent: A Season of Surprises, he turns his attention to the surprising people involved in the gospel stories surrounding Christmas, and, in the process, he helps us see ourselves in those characters. Advent: A Season of Surprises is a meaningful Advent study!

Adam Hamilton
Pastor and author of Wrestling with Doubt and Finding Faith

In Advent: A Season of Surprises, Scott Chrostek reminds us Advent isn't just a nostalgic story about the past. It's a glimpse into the future God desires for us. God came into the world so humanity could come into the presence of God. For those who seek God's presence this Advent, I can think of no better place to start than by discovering the reality of the God who comes to us in Christ, calls us to love, and cares for us completely in the pages of Advent: A Season of Surprises.

Wil Cantrell
Pastor and author of ATONE and From Heaven to Earth

The weeks before Christmas are filled with decorating, planning for travel or company, thinking about food, making lists, and checking them twice. Traditionally the Church has also intended these to be days of deep reflection. Scott Chrostek is a delightful guide to this season of the year, offering profound meditations on a God who arrives into the world and into our lives in surprising ways. Like composing a good song, Chrostek begins with familiar themes but helps us hear them in new ways. This book is its own sonic journey toward Christmas, to be read with joy and anticipation.

Bishop David A. Bard
Michigan Conference of The United Methodist Church

As a pre-Christmas study, Advent: A Season of Surprises will give each reader (and class member) multiple reasons to feel good. Everybody knows the story, and we all like familiar things. Thankfully, in a world of calendar-shattering change, the Christmas story feels like an oasis of familiarity – until it isn't. Scott Chrostek has a way of taking you where you never expected to go while teaching you things that no one has helped you to learn. And more than once, you'll hear yourself saying, "I never saw that coming." Beginning with Scott's opening pages, the key word is "surprise." But as a gnarled and wizened old preacher, I still like surprises. And I join Scott in trusting that you will also.

Dr. William A. Ritter
Pastor Emeritus at First United Methodist Church, Birmingham, Michigan

The Christmas story is so familiar that it is easy to miss its power. But this book will help you see the story with fresh eyes. Moving seamlessly from scripture to Christmas music to everyday life, Chrostek illuminates just how surprising the Christmas story was and still is for us today. Whether you pick it up for yourself, a small group, or a Sunday School class, this book will help you and your people see the familiar story in a new way.

Matt Miofsky
Lead Pastor, The Gathering, Saint Louis, Missouri

Made in the USA
Coppell, TX
05 November 2024

39669994R00072